FIX IT! How to Repair Automotive Dents, Scratches, Tears and Stains

By Kris Palmer
Photography By Jerry Lee

motorbooks

First published in 2011 by Motorbooks, an imprint of MBI Publishing Company, 400 First Avenue North, Suite 300, Minneapolis, MN 55401 USA

The information in this book is true and complete to the best of our knowledge. All recommendations are made without any guarantee on the part of the author or Publisher, who also disclaims any liability incurred in connection with the use of this data or specific details.

We recognize, further, that some words, model names, and designations mentioned herein are the property of the trademark holder. We use them for identification purposes only. This is not an official publication.

Motorbooks titles are also available at discounts in bulk quantity for industrial or sales-promotional use. For details write to Special Sales Manager at MBI Publishing Company, 400 First Avenue North, Suite 300, Minneapolis, MN 55401 USA.

To find out more about our books, visit us online at www.motorbooks.com.

ISBN-13: 978-0-7603-3989-3

Library of Congress Cataloging-in-Publication Data

Palmer, Kris E., 1964–
 Fix it! : how to repair automotive scratches, dents, tears and stains / Kris Palmer ; photography by Jerry Lee. — 1st ed.
    p. cm.
 ISBN 978-0-7603-3989-3 (sb)
   1.   Automobiles—Bodies—Maintenance and repair—Amateurs' manuals. I. Title.
 TL255.P35 2011
 629.2'60288—dc22
                    2010041980

President/CEO: Ken Fund
Publisher: Zack Miller
Editors: Peter Schletty and Jeffrey Zuehlke
Creative Director: Michele Lanci-Altomare
Design Manager: Brad Springer
Designer: Heather Parlato

Printed in China

On the front cover: top left: Sean Clarkson/Alamy; top right: Motoring Picture Library/Alamy; bottom left: © Cy Furlan; bottom right: iStockphoto
On the frontis piece: *Shutterstock*
On the title page: *Shutterstock*
Photos on pages 11, 30, 70, 112: *Shutterstock*

Contents

ABOUT THE AUTHOR

Kris Palmer has pondered and tinkered with cars since he was a wee lad and has written about them for over a decade for the *Minneapolis Star Tribune*. He is the author of *Dream Garages, The Fast and the Furious: The Official Car Guide, Survivor: The Unrestored Collector Car,* and *Motorcycle Survivor*. His writing also appears in *The Cobra in the Barn, The Vincent in the Barn, Motorcycle Dream Garages, The Devil Can Ride, How to Repair Your Car,* and *How to Repair Your Pickup or SUV*. He also practices law and lives in Minneapolis with his wife of 15 years, Jenneane Jansen. He owns a Triumph TR6 (car), an MGB GT, an Audi S4, and a Honda CB1100F.

ABOUT THE PHOTOGRAPHER

Jerry Lee's arresting images of cars, motorcycles, athletes, and models have enhanced books, magazines, and newspapers for 28 years. Jerry's sharp, detailed photographs have appeared in *Sports Illustrated, NCAA News,* Kris Palmer's *Survivor: The Unrestored Collector Car,* and *Motorcycle Survivor: Tips and Tales in the Unrestored Realm*; Motorbooks International's *How to Repair Your Car* and *How to Repair Your SUV*; as well as many other publications. Jerry makes his home in Cottage Grove, Minnesota, with wife Loretta, daughter Megan, and Takoda, the golden doodle dog.

ACKNOWLEDGMENTS

Warmest thanks to the Newgate Education Center for welcoming me and ace photographer Jerry Lee into their facility to perform and photograph the projects for this book. Newgate provides auto body, paint, and mechanics training to young people and adults in need of marketable skills. The center is funded by donated vehicles, which students repair and paint as needed. Donors receive a tax deduction and repaired vehicles are either auctioned off or re-donated to needy recipients.

Special thanks to Gary, Don, and Dennis for their help, enthusiasm, and expertise. Check out Newgate Education Center online at www.newgateschool.org or in person at 2900 East Hennepin Avenue, Minneapolis, MN 55413, phone 612-378-0177.

Tools and Safety

As proven by the popular "Darwin Awards"—given to people who remove themselves from the gene pool in foolish ways—it's possible to get hurt doing virtually anything. The projects in this book are not dangerous, nor are they difficult. They will go more smoothly, however, if you approach the tools you use and your vehicle with care.

Every tool has a purpose and one or two effective ways to use it. They can also be misused, often to the tool's and the user's detriment. Correct use keeps the tool squarely on the part it's designed to tighten or remove or adjust. Ad-libbed uses sometimes work, but they also create the risk that the tool will slip off, mar the head of the screw or bolt at issue, bend or break something non-expendable, fly into a hand, leg, or beautifully painted fender, or propel the wielding hand itself into something always harder, usually sharp and often rusty (an event mechanics call a "knuckle-buster").

When using wrenches or screwdrivers, pick one that fits the fastener snugly. With a screwdriver, press the tool into the slot firmly and at the same angle as the screw. Tighten adjustable wrenches down onto the nut or bolt head so there is no play; turn the wrench in the same plane as the nut, rather than off angle—if it slips under force, it will round off the bolt-head's edges and make it much harder to remove.

Pliers (square or needle-nose) are handy for grabbing, pulling and holding parts, but they will chew up a nut or bolt—especially if they are not locking pliers (e.g., Vice-Grips). You're better off using a wrench—adjustable, open-end, or socket—to grasp or turn nuts and bolts, particularly ones you plan to reuse.

A few of the projects within this book recommend using a razorblade to scrape off a sticker or residue. This very useful tool must be used—and stored—with maximum common sense. After you scrape something, put the blade back in its cardboard protector and set it in a safe, known spot, like a flat corner of the top tray on your tool box. Don't set it on your car seat or dashboard or some other random spot, such as an ashtray you'll later reach into!

Power tools deserve our respect. Many an experienced mechanic and craftsperson has a scar from a powered tool handled with momentary inattention. Grasp them firmly, keep your eyes on the work you're doing with them, wear safety goggles to protect your eyes. Read the manufacturer's instructions, too, including all precautions. There are tools you want to use gloves with, like a welder, and some you don't. A friend of the author's broke his finger when he was using a router with gloves on (in winter) and the router grabbed the glove.

Finally, respect the vehicle itself, even at rest. Gravity has an unwavering affection for cars and trucks and will pull them off ramps and jacks and down inclines—and at people—at the first opportunity. Automobiles also hold mischievous fluids and gases. Oil, brake fluid, transmission fluid, and radiator fluid are slick and toxic. Gasoline fumes are flammable, and exhaust is deadly. Battery acid is caustic and its fumes are explosive. Metal edges, like a fender's, can be sharp, and the rust that forms under almost all vehicles will wait with a stalactite's patience to fall into your eye when you crawl underneath (wear safety goggles).

We're not trying to scare you—the purpose of this book is to get more pleasure from your vehicle. Be smart, use common sense, keep yourself and others out of harm's way, and you'll be happy to see all the useful things you can accomplish with some simple tools and your best efforts.

Shutterstock

Introduction

After a house, an automobile is among our most expensive purchases. College and graduate school rank up there, too, for those who pursue them, but the point is that new cars and trucks cost big money. When the green paper is in short supply, we make our lives more sustainable and less stressful by holding onto our current vehicle instead of incurring a long-term car payment.

Fix It! will benefit any vehicle and may be especially welcome for owners seeking a few more years out of their current ride. The projects within make vehicles more comfortable, convenient, and attractive so that holding onto that dependable 10- or 15-year-old car or truck feels good—an exercise in logic and prudence. And the better an older vehicle looks, the more appealing and valuable it seems and the less concern we have in continuing to rely on it, wherever we need to go.

In these pages, we explain 40 projects to fix up and dress up your vehicle. They are within the competence of any driver, with photos and captions to help you see and understand how to get the job done. Section 1 will give your vehicle's exterior a basic cleanup, showing you what you can do and how easy it is to make your car look better. In Section 2 we move inside to allow passengers to be just as impressed with your efforts as passers-by. We get a bit more technical with the projects in Part 3—though there is nothing here you cannot accomplish! Part 4 gets your glass and mirrors in shape to improve your own perspective. Finally, Part 5 offers several further projects for your comfort and convenience.

As you work through the book, you will realize that there are many things you can do to improve your car's appearance and condition. Sometimes understanding the basic skills and knowing you can master them is the most important knowledge of all. Thank you for making *Fix It!* part of your automotive library. May it serve you well and inspire you to take on other projects to make your life easier and more cost-effective.

—Kris Palmer, Spring 2011

How to Use this Book

 Skill Level: Fix It!'s projects can benefit any vehicle and do not require advanced training or skills. All of the projects in this book are either "easy" or "intermediate" level. The latter type are slightly more involved and time-consuming than the easy projects, but within the abilities of the average vehicle owner.

 Tools/Supplies Required: this list is representative for the project. Individual tools may vary—e.g., screwdriver or wrench—depending on the fastener type your manufacturer selected.

 Time Required: an estimate of the minutes you will need to complete the project.

 Cost Estimate: what you can expect to spend to complete each project. If you have a well-stocked garage, many projects will have no cost beyond your time and "shop supplies." Otherwise the vast majority are inexpensive to perform compared with typical repair shop costs.

Shutterstock

SECTION 1
BODY CLEANUP

Think of your close friends, neighbors, and co-workers. Know what they drive? Bet you do. Our vehicles are a reflection of ourselves—one we can make clearer and more appealing. In this section, we examine simple ways to make our vehicles look better. Once you perform these projects, you'll be ready for further ways to improve your car or truck in later sections.

PROJECT 1
Cleaning the Engine Bay

 Skill Level: easy

 Tools/Supplies Required: hose, engine de-greaser, plastic bag, tape/rope/small bungee to seal off alternator

 Time Required: 15 minutes

 Parts Source: auto parts store

 Cost Estimate: under $10

Something about a dirty engine gives us pause, whether in working on our own car or considering buying a used one. "What is all that grease hiding?" "Can I even touch that engine—to check the oil, top up washer fluid, or replace the air filter—without leaving greasy fingerprints wherever I go afterward?"

A clean engine is inviting and, luckily, not difficult to achieve. Just use a spray-on engine cleaner. The best place to do this is at a do-it-yourself car wash where the chemicals will be caught by the facility's waste-water system. When working with chemicals, wear gloves and safety glasses to protect your eyes and skin.

Do you want to work under this hood? Not yet....

Not every part benefits from liberal application of cleaner or water. The alternator, distributor, and coil-on-plug ignition in this Geo may perform poorly if doused with liquid. One approach is to avoid spraying cleaner or water directly at the components. Another option, as done here, is to cover the alternator and distributor with plastic.

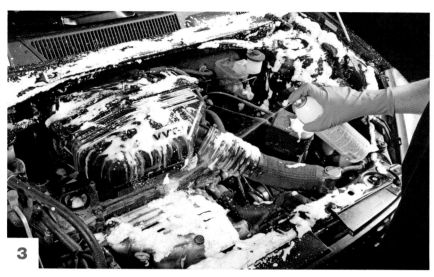

Off-the-shelf engine cleaners include spray foams like this product from Gunk. Read the label first to understand the best method of use. This product, for example, works best starting with a dry, cool engine. Spray it on liberally so it can loosen up accumulated grease.

This foam cleaner is a spray-on-rinse-off product. We're using a car-wash-style wand here. Its powerful stream is useful in most areas, though we would not spray it directly into the alternator or at the distributor.

Now the engine doesn't look like something we want to avoid.

PROJECT 2
Cleaning/Polishing Chrome

 Skill Level: easy

 Tools/Supplies Required: soft rag, chrome cleaning spray or liquid

Time Required: 15 minutes

Parts Source: auto parts store

 Cost Estimate: under $10

Chrome seems to come and go on cars, disappearing when it gets too common and reappearing when the all-color look grows old. Keep in mind when you have a car with chrome that what lies underneath may not be steel. If it's a classic car's chrome wheel or bumper, it probably is, but many trim parts, like grilles and badges, have for decades been made of plastic.

Both types may be cleaned and polished, but plastic pieces are not as strong as their metal counterparts and must be approached with care so you don't scratch or break them. Be sure of what you're dealing with before taking anything abrasive to the chrome on your car. For example, with a chromed-steel wheel or bumper, fine steel wool works great for removing light oxidation. Steel wool, even at its finest grade, is risky with chromed plastic, however. You're better off trying a soft sponge or cloth and a mild cleaner that is labeled to be safe on plastics.

1

The chrome piece at the rear of this Volvo would surprise many a classic car fan. Despite its location by the bumper, it is a plastic part.

This spray cleaner is a detailing product that is safe with plastic parts. You can find such products at any auto parts store. We sprayed it on liberally to loosen up grime.

Use a soft rag with the cleaner to wipe away the dirt. If you drop the rag on the ground, get a new one (and wash the dropped one so that grit from the ground doesn't scratch your vehicle).

The part looks a lot better cleaned and polished. It isn't quite show quality, though. The chrome on this plastic is starting to show its age, particularly below the seam beneath the taillight where water has flowed down onto it for many years. If you had a part similar to this and it was too tired to clean up well, you could always prep it with fine sandpaper and paint it a semi-gloss black to match the bumper. (See Project 35 for an example of fixing a deteriorated plastic coating with paint.)

PROJECT 3
Restoring Discolored Headlight Lenses

 Skill Level: easy, but requires elbow grease if done without power tools

 Tools/Supplies Required: rags, fine sandpaper, rubbing compound

 Time Required: 30 to 45 minutes

 Parts Source: auto parts store

 Cost Estimate: $10 - $25

Most modern headlights utilize a replaceable bulb that shines through a glass or plastic lens. Exposure to the sun and the elements can cause this lens to become hazy and opaque, decreasing headlight efficiency and making the vehicle look prematurely old.

Depending on the vehicle, the housing containing the lens can be expensive, difficult to find, or both. The good news is that the hazy lens can be polished to remove the exterior discoloration and deterioration and be virtually as clear as it was when the car was new. This work can be done by hand with very fine sandpaper and polish, or it can be accomplished with a handheld buffer. Either way, the results are outstanding and well worth the effort. The materials for this project are available at automotive parts and paint supply stores.

1

Compared to the adjacent turn-signal lens, this headlight looks bad—as if it had been hauled up from the bottom of a pond.

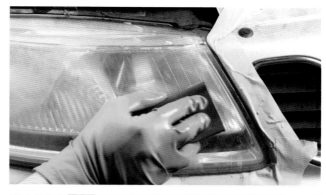

2

Because we'll be using abrasives, albeit mild, let's tape off the surrounding paint to avoid scuffing it up as we work.

3

On a lens this opaque, we started out with 1500 grit wet sandpaper and then moved up to 2000 grit, applying moderate, even pressure and varied circular motion to "cut" the full exterior lens surface evenly. Use plenty of water and wipe the lens with a rag regularly so you can see how you're doing.

4

The last wet sanding we did was with 3000 grit paper on a backing pad.

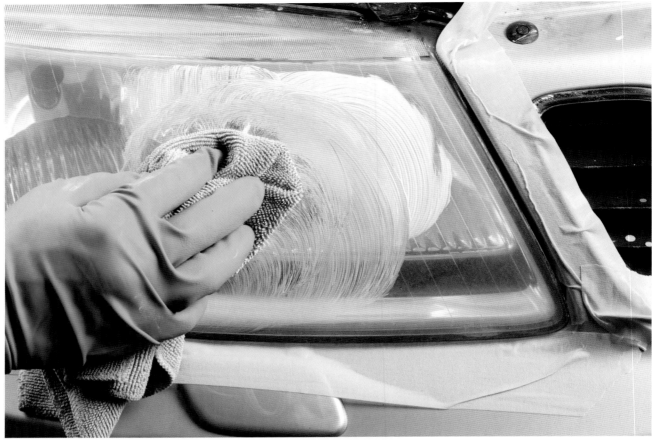

For the final stage, we used rubbing compound for that extra degree of polish. You can buy a headlight refinishing kit in stores and online that provides everything you'll need for the job. Some are designed for a high-speed drill (or buffer if you have one) to minimize elbow grease. The principle will be the same—polish down through the crud to get back to a nice, clear lens.

The refinished lens is back to its original look, just as clear and transparent as the turn-signal lens we used as an initial benchmark. Remove tape and we're done.

PROJECT 4
Cleaning out Leaves and Debris

 Skill Level: easy

 Time Required: 15 to 45 minutes

Tools/Supplies Required: screwdriver, pliers, ratchet (depending on your vehicle's fasteners)

 Parts Source: auto parts store

 Cost Estimate: $0 (or the price of any fasteners that get broken, probably under $10)

If you live in an area with trees and your vehicle spends any meaningful time outside, leaves can collect in large quantity not only in obvious compartments, like the bed of a pickup, but in smaller, less noticeable nooks too. For example, on many vehicles there is a gap at the base of the windshield that may contain water drainage, air intake passageways, and components for the windshield wiper system.

Accumulated leaves can block drain and intake passageways, holding moisture, disrupting airflow, and promoting rust and other problems. Rodents may also find a hidden bed of leaves a nice place to raise a family,

particularly if you leave the car idle for a while, such as during winter storage.

Plastic panels may block our view of accumulated leaves, as well as our access for removing them. These panels and the fasteners that secure them can become brittle over time and may prove easier to break than replace. They're also easy to misplace on blacktop or in a garage. As you remove them, keep track of where each fastener came from and how it went in. Do this with metal fasteners too. An easy approach is to set them out on, say, a workbench with positions that correspond to their location on the vehicle.

A panel at the base of this VW Golf's windshield obscured a large cavity where leaves slowly accumulated. Removing these fasteners required a Phillips screwdriver. On other cars, these fasteners may require a slotted screwdriver or a different kind of tool. Remove them carefully to avoid breakage.

Rotting leaves are messy. Before you start removing them, find a bucket or other suitable container to hold them so you don't create more work for yourself with a second mess.

You can scoop the leaves out by hand and also flush the area with a hose. A wet/dry shop vac will pull out any pieces that remain.

PROJECT 5
Washing Your Car

 Skill Level: easy

 Tools/Supplies Required: sponge, bucket, car-wash soap, towels, chamois (optional)

 Time Required: 15 to 30 minutes

 Parts Source: auto parts store

Cost Estimate: under $10 per wash

This is one of this book's simplest projects. Yet keeping your vehicle clean is important in several ways. Removing impurities and debris like spilled foods or chemicals, sap, tar, and bird droppings will keep the finish in better condition longer. Appearances count when you resell the vehicle or, if you're unfortunate enough to get in an accident, when an insurance adjuster looks at it. A car that appears in excellent condition will command a higher price than one that looks faded and generally uncared for. Besides, you'll feel better pulling up to work, leisure activities, and your friends' homes in a car that looks good.

There are many products out there for washing cars. Any car-wash soap and a bucket and sponge will work fine. Some people use dish soap, but detailing pros advise against it. Dishes are not metal, they're not painted, and the "contaminant" to be removed from them is food, not dirt, bugs, salt, etc. A product designed to clean car paint should yield better long-term results.

Be sure to hose down the vehicle first. This will loosen up dirt and dust and make the washing easier. Start high on the vehicle and wash from the top down. The worst dirt and grit will be down near the tires and the road. Wash that area last to avoid rubbing that grit into the paint on the rest of the car.

Our tendency when we wash something is to use hot water, yet this is not necessary—on cool days it's even undesirable because it will cause the metal and paint to expand rapidly, stressing the finish. Try lukewarm water. It will work fine and won't burn your hands.

The area behind the tires gets especially dirty, so wash thoroughly here at all four wheels.

Rinse the vehicle again after washing it and then give it a good looking over to see if you've gotten the car clean throughout. It's easy to leave a little band of dirt if you're not careful, and we want that gone . . . because we're also going to wax your proud ride in the next project.

To finish the job and avoid water spots, use a chamois or some old towels to dry the car. You can keep your gloves on for this or, if your hands are getting hot, take them off. There's no threat to them in drying a clean car.

PROJECT 6
Waxing Your Car

 Skill Level: easy

 Tools/Supplies Required: clean, soft rags, car wax

 Time Required: 30 minutes

 Parts Source: auto parts store

 Cost Estimate: under $15

It's so easy to wash the car and be done. Sometimes that's OK—it all takes time, and in our busy world, time can be hard to come by. Every time you remove dirt and corrosive agents, you're doing your vehicle's finish a favor. But at least twice a year—like end of fall and start of summer—it's important to put down a good coat of wax.

Washing your car to make it clean is beneficial. But waxing it provides a protective layer between that clean paint and all of the chemicals and forces seeking to break it down. That layer helps to keep that paint beautiful for many years. Wax is like clothing or sunscreen for your car or truck—it's there for protection from salt, bird droppings, airborne pollutants, and the sun's powerful rays.

Car wax will not harm your skin, so wear or don't wear gloves as you wish.

There are a dizzying number of car-care products on the market. Don't let them overwhelm you. If you aren't prepping your vehicle for some major auto show—and maybe even then—using car wax of any kind is more important than which one you use. Ask a neighbor with a nice-looking car or a clerk at the auto parts store for a trusty car wax. Waxes that contain abrasives may make light scratches in clear-coated finishes.

Apply the wax as the manufacturer recommends—typically with a soft, clean cloth or the applicator included with the product. Using a circular motion to cover every painted panel is the age-old method. Some waxes may not be recommended for plastic, so read the label. If you drop the cloth on the ground, get a new one so you don't rub abrasive dirt into your finish or get it in your wax.

Once you've waxed every appropriate painted surface, use a fresh soft cloth to remove the excess wax. You will feel it glide over the paint—that's the protective layer you've just provided. It will add beautiful shine and make water run off like it's afraid to be on there.

The finished product: washed and waxed and ready to face life's environmental challenges. The two faint lines on the hood are light scratches. They can be buffed out with the techniques shown in Projects 23 and 24.

PROJECT 7

Removing Faded and/or Deteriorating Pinstriping

 Skill Level: intermediate (some basic tool experience useful but not necessary)

Tools/Supplies Required: fingernail, plastic spatula (heat gun may help)

 Time Required: 15 to 45 minutes

Parts Source: auto parts store

Cost Estimate: under $10

Pinstripes can add a unique touch to a car. On modern cars these stripes tend to be plastic strips rather than the old-school hand-painted lines. If you wish to replace a pinstripe that has faded or started to peel, or to remove one from a replacement fender you've bought that does not match the rest of the car, you'll find that these plastic strips are not too difficult to remove. On the other hand, a painted pinstripe would most likely need to be sanded off and the whole panel repainted.

In many cases, you can simply peel a plastic stripe off by carefully getting under it with a thin implement such as a plastic spatula that won't scratch the paint underneath. If its hold on the panel is too strong, you can use a hairdryer or heat gun to soften the adhesive and loosen it up.

This replacement fender was a remarkably close match to the original car's 14-year-old paint. It's pinstriped, however, which is an instant giveaway that it's a swapped-in part, because the other panels have no stripes. (The wax-pencil mark is from the salvage yard, presumably indicating that the part came in on April 18 and is from a 1997 model. It will fit our 1996 Golf just fine.)

Some fingernail scraping got the job started, but not everyone uses their nails as tools. This plastic spatula was strong enough to peel off the stripe without making scratches.

Because the unstriped portion was exposed to more sun, there's a faint ghost mark where each stripe once resided, but it's a much cleaner look than before. Time, polishing, and waxing will make the stripe's former location less noticeable.

Lacquer thinner on a rag removed the salvage yard's mark for a clean fender. Always wear rubber gloves when working with solvents.

PROJECT 8
Removing Stickers and Decals

 Skill Level: easy

 Tools/Supplies Required: razorblade (scrape handle optional), citrus "goo remover," heat gun or hair dryer

 Time Required: 5 to 15 minutes

 Parts Source: auto parts store

 Cost Estimate: $0–$15

Political views, sports teams, our alma mater . . . all topics that find their way onto our vehicles in the form of stickers and decals. But views change, vehicles change hands, and eventually these tiny message boards begin to look old and shabby. They'll come off though, with patience and the right technique.

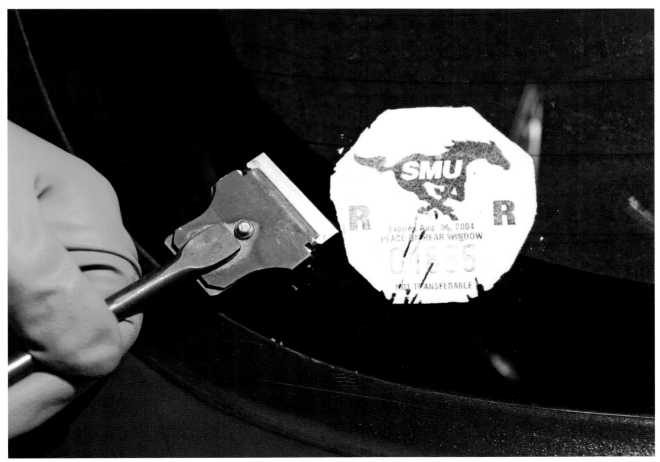

A sticker on glass can be scraped off with a razorblade. Use a single-edge blade. Auto parts stores sell scrapers like this, which will hold the blade for you for more control. For a sticker on paint, such as a trunk lid or bumper, don't use a razorblade.

27

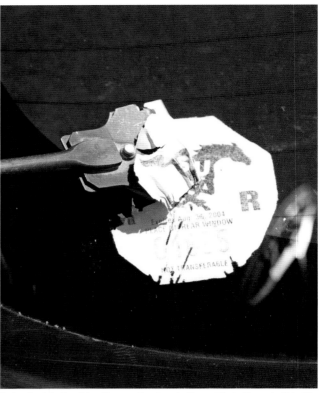

Hold the blade down onto the glass at an oblique angle and press it with a smooth, controlled motion into the sticker. Never push a sharp tool toward flesh. It's most efficient to peel the sticker off in large pieces. Peel up a corner with your fingernail and use goo remover, or a heat gun or hair dryer, to weaken the adhesive.

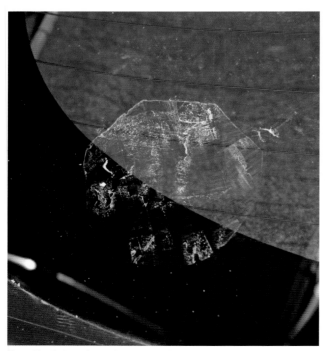

The residue that remains can be removed with glass cleaner or a citrus "goo remover."

Decals are popular glass accoutrements that go on and come off even more easily. This one is on the inside of the glass.

Get a fingernail under one corner of the decal and pull.

Do so in a controlled manner to make sure the decal, and only the decal, pulls loose. Modern decals adhere without adhesive, so once it's off, there's nothing more to do—other than see better out the back window.

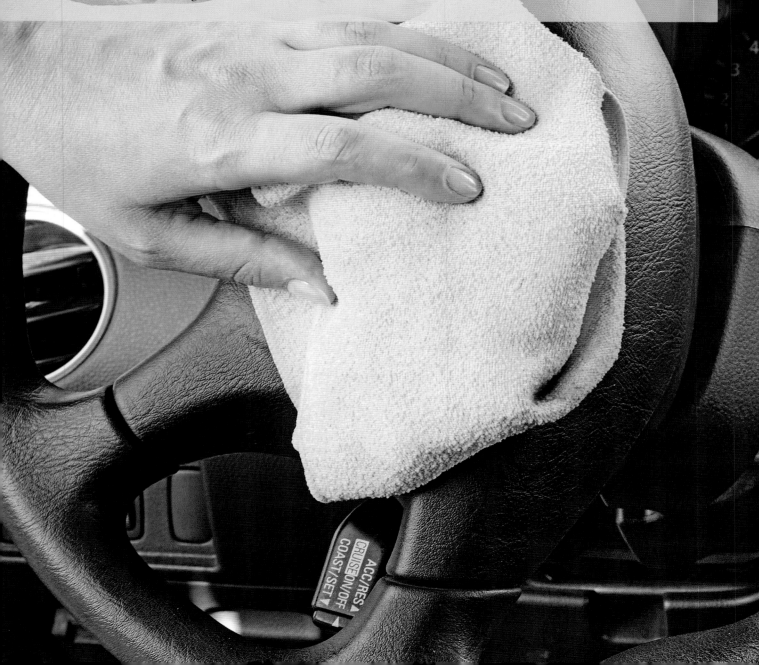

SECTION 2
REFRESHING THE INTERIOR

The interior shelters us from rain, snow, sleet, hail, high winds, bitter cold, and raging heat. It doesn't go unscathed, however, because we cause damage over time just like the elements do outside. Spilled foods, beverages, chemicals, greasy fingers, pets, dirt, grit, sand—even our clothing—will cause wear, stains, rips, and grunge. With the right tools, products, and a little effort, we can remove much of this tarnish and decay and make the interior look newer and more inviting.

PROJECT 9
Re-Coloring Worn Leather with Leather Crème

 Skill Level: easy

Tools/Supplies Required: soft rag, leather crème

 Time Required: 15 to 30 minutes

 Parts Source: auto parts store

 Cost Estimate: under $10

Unlike the other seats in a car, the driver's seat gets no relief. Any time the vehicle is used, the material covering the driver's seat gets stressed, flexed, and abraded. Eventually, it will show wear even in the most expensive automobiles. A leather steering wheel faces the same relentless contact.

Fortunately, leather care products are abundant and time-tested. In the photos that follow, we show two ways to restore color to worn leather. We have used products manufactured by shoe care companies, though saddle shops and specialty car companies carry the same types of products. All are designed to treat leather that has been subjected to heavy stresses.

This side panel gets scuffed and flexed every time the driver settles into the seat. Relentless chafing and flexing have worn off the grey color this seat had when new.

This shoe crème matches the upholstery color so closely, it could have been made by Volvo!

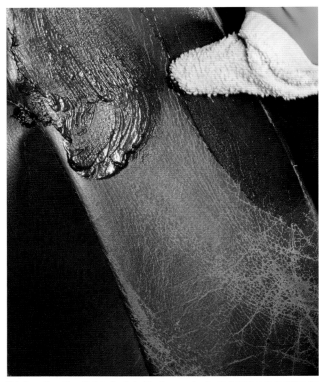

Rub the crème liberally into the faded leather, moving in all directions to coat the discolored areas completely.

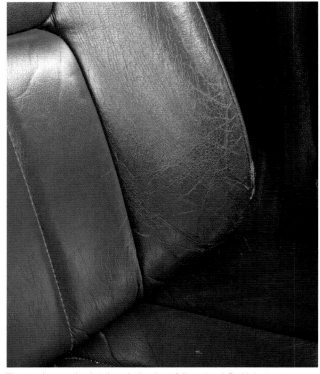

After the leather has been uniformly re-colored, use a clean, soft cloth to remove any excess, and polish the crème to a satin gloss. Be sure to reach the cloth into creases and seams so no lingering crème poses a stain threat to the occupant's clothing.

The creasing remains, but the color has been fully restored. For high-stress areas like this, you may need to reapply it periodically. Alternatively, you can dye the leather as we do in the next project.

PROJECT 10
Dyeing Interior Leather

 Skill Level: easy

 Time Required: 15 to 45 minutes

Tools/Supplies Required: leather dye, rags

 Parts Source: auto parts store

Cost Estimate: $5–$25

Our previous project showed how leather crème can bring scuffed leather back to its original look and color. Leather dye will also restore the color and is more resistant to being worn off. In this project, we again treated the edge of a driver's seat, which sees contact every time the car is used. We also treated a leather steering wheel, which experiences wear from drivers' hands and steering motions and from any rings drivers may wear.

The leather on the car we used for this project happened to be black, which can be easier to match or blend than other colors. Before you commit and treat a highly visible area, try your dye in an inconspicuous spot, like the lower front driver's seat, to make sure it's a good match. Some manufacturers and aftermarket suppliers offer dyes that are blended to match particular interior colors.

The leather wheel on this Audi has lost its deep black color in the areas where drivers' hands and jewelry made most frequent and forceful contact.

Conveniently, the leather's worn areas—where the original finish is compromised—are more receptive to stain. We used a shoe-based leather dye. Application requires depressing the foam applicator onto the leather, which opens a small valve and lets the dye flow into the applicator foam.

We treated the whole wheel—not just the worn areas—to make the finished color as even as possible.

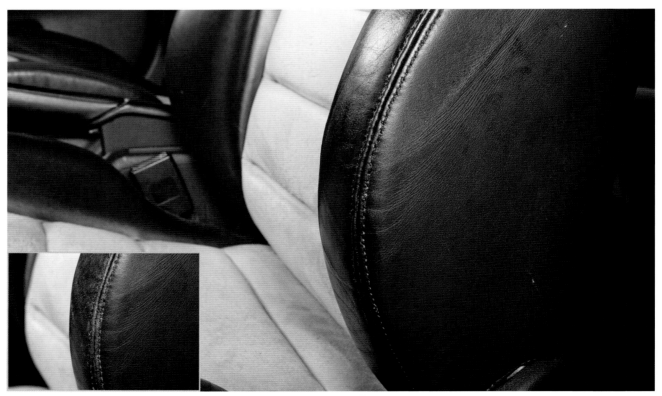

We also treated the outside edge of the driver's seat, where friction from drivers' clothing had left its mark.

PROJECT 11
Cleaning Leather Upholstery

 Skill Level: easy

 Time Required: 15 minutes

Tools/Supplies Required: upholstery cleaner, rags

 Parts Source: auto parts store

 Cost Estimate: $15

Leather is a durable, breathable material that has served as a seating surface for thousands of years. Properly cared for, it will last decades or longer. It may cost a lot more than cloth, but it's worth the price.

In this project, we are going to remove a stain from a spilled liquid that has dried out on this passenger seat. It's best to remove any spill quickly to avoid a permanent stain or damage if the spill is a corrosive agent.

A liquid was spilled on this leather passenger seat and has now dried to bright white. Leather cleaner will help remove it without posing a threat of its own to the upholstery.

For best results, follow the product manufacturer's directions. In this case, the manufacturer advises spraying the cleaner on a rag and then wiping away the stain.

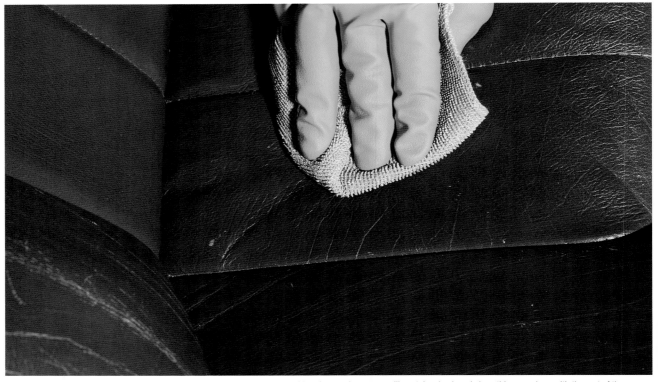

Liquids will follow gravity to the gap between the backrest and bottom seat cushion. As you clean up a spill or stain, check and clean this area along with the rest of the affected upholstery.

This stain cleaned up without a trace. Even when some of the stain remains, it will still look much better than before.

PROJECT 12
Conditioning Leather Upholstery

 Skill Level: easy

 Tools/Supplies Required: leather conditioner, rags

 Time Required: 15 minutes

 Parts Source: auto parts store

Cost Estimate: under $15

Upholstery leather can dry out over the years and eventually crack. Leather conditioners keep this type of upholstery supple for decades of use, should the rest of the vehicle last so long.

Sometimes conditioner is combined with cleaner, making care of your leather upholstery as simple as it can be.

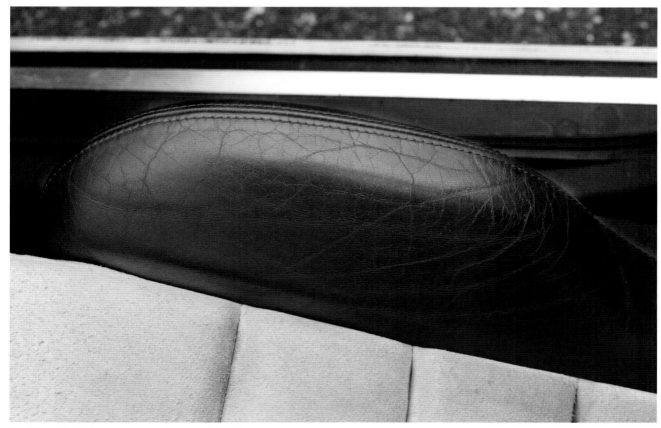

Even high-quality leather requires care to stay clean and supple.

Whether your conditioner is a spray or crème, apply it as the manufacturer recommends. This version sprays on.

With a crème, you will typically use a soft rag to apply it evenly to the leather surface, using enough for it to penetrate the leather and then removing any excess so it doesn't get on your clothing later.

The conditioned leather shines and looks closer to new.

PROJECT 13
Cleaning Interior Vinyl

 Skill Level: easy

 Tools/Supplies Required: vinyl cleaner, rags

 Time Required: 15 to 45 minutes

 Parts Source: auto parts store

Cost Estimate: $5–$15

Automobiles transport not only people, but all of the stuff we tote around, including food and beverages. Some of these solids and liquids, along with dust, dirt, and pet hair, find their way into our vehicles, leaving a dirty or greasy film or stain.

A mild detergent on a damp rag will clean up much of this grime. Upholstery cleaner made for vinyl will also do the job. A vinyl detailing spray will provide a deeper-looking shine.

There is both wear and dirt here. The wear we can't reverse, but we can make the vinyl look much better.

We used an all-purpose foam cleaner from the auto parts store, along with a clean terry cloth rag.

The rag works well on the flat areas.

For seams and creases, a brush can remove dirt beyond a rag's reach. This is a brush that would be suitable for shoes—stiff but not too stiff. A wire brush would be too harsh; it would leave scratches or gouges.

In addition to the cleaner, we tried a detailing spray specifically for vinyl. The cleaner alone provided a great look; it's up to you whether you want to go for a little extra shine.

PROJECT 14
Cleaning Cloth Upholstery

 Skill Level: easy

 Tools/Supplies Required: upholstery cleaner, rags, brush (optional)

 Time Required: 15 to 45 minutes

 Parts Source: auto parts store

 Cost Estimate: $5–$15

The synthetic cloth upholstery in modern automobiles resists staining. With time and use, it will become soiled, however. Common substances like coffee and grease have a knack for finding light-colored cloth interiors and leaving their mark.

A foaming cleaner used with a brush or textured rag will remove most of the dirt and stains. We used a product designed for automotive upholstery and carpet. Such products are available at most auto parts stores and department stores that carry automotive supplies.

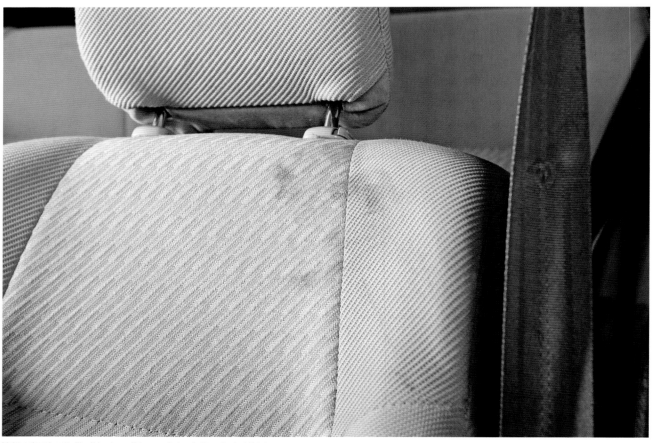

Light-colored seats like this show dirt more obviously than do dark fabrics.

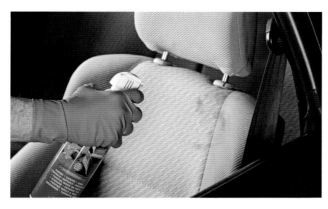

We sprayed the foam directly at the stain.

Hit the whole stained area with foam spray.

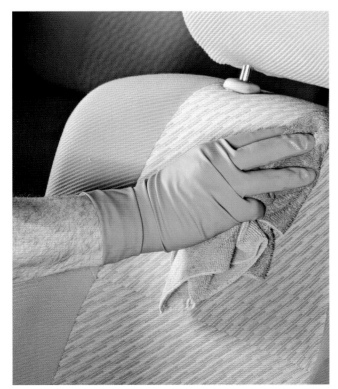

Brisk scrubbing with a terry cloth rag helped the cleaner do its best. Virtually all of the stain came out.

The top of the seat now looks great, but...

...the bottom of the seat is also soiled.

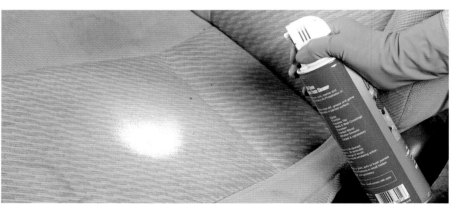

Same treatment here: a good dose of foam cleaner, followed by scrubbing with a clean terry cloth rag.

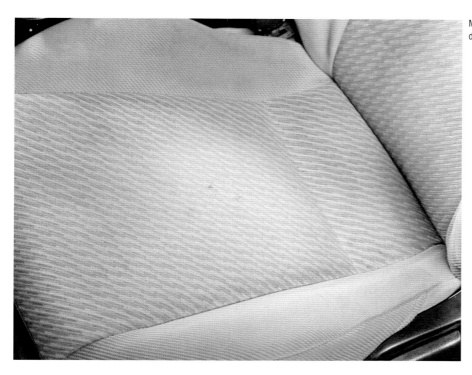

Most of the stain came out. The seat is still a little damp here, which is darkening the fabric.

When it dries fully the result will look better with a more even color.

PROJECT 15
Repairing a Torn Seat

 Skill Level: intermediate

 Tools/Supplies Required: leather needle, upholstery thread, small pliers

 Time Required: 30 minutes to 1.5 hours

 Parts Source: department/discount store

 Cost Estimate: under $20

Seat materials are chosen and developed for resistance to wear and tears. Objects that are heavy or sharp will tear them, however, and seams will give way before the material itself fails. How difficult it is to repair depends on the extent and location of the tear.

Whether to undertake the repair yourself depends on how professional you want the result to look. You can take it to an auto upholstery shop for a flawless repair, or you can do your best and get some satisfaction out of tackling it yourself for a lot less money. Naturally, that's the route we're going to take for this project. A final alternative is to find, purchase, and install a good used seat for the vehicle. You can do this through a salvage yard or online. See project 16.

The leather on this Audi seat is still good, but the seam has failed. For an inexpensive home repair, we're going to sew it ourselves.

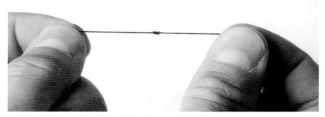

Proper thread is critical—it has to be strong synthetic thread made for upholstery. General purpose thread from the sewing box at home won't be strong enough to do the job. You'll also need a bigger knot so it won't pull through. Looping the thread many times rather than just once is a good start. If you need it bigger still because it pulls through, carefully make one or more additional knots on top of the first one.

Do this repair safely by following these precautions. First, **protect your eyesight with eyeglasses or safety glasses, because the needle can break and fly up at you.** Second, use a thimble so the needle goes into the upholstery rather than your fingertip. Third, use a sturdy needle with a sturdy eye (where the thread goes) to resist breakage. The eye on this needle was thin and elongated, and it broke. Finally, push straight; flexing the needle will break it.

Start sewing where the seam is still good to one side of the opening. For the cleanest look, we tried to duplicate what the manufacturer did, using their holes or at least putting any new ones in line with them. We zigzagged behind the open seam without looping the thread across the top of it to keep the same look as before.

You may need a small pliers to pull the needle out from the other side of tough leather. After you pull the needle through, pull on the thread to snug each stitch so it pulls the seam closed.

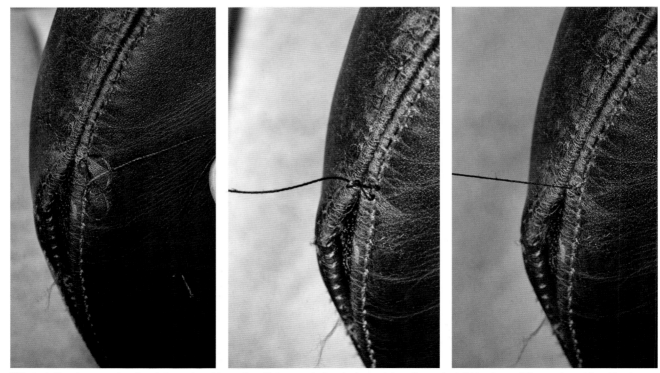

With sturdy thread, you can close the whole opening with one piece. That may make it easier for you to keep the repair straight and even. If the one piece of thread breaks, however, you may have to undo part or all of your repair to knot it down. We made one knot part way along to "finalize" that section. Just loop the thread on itself a couple times and pull the knot tight. Now you can start a new piece of thread.

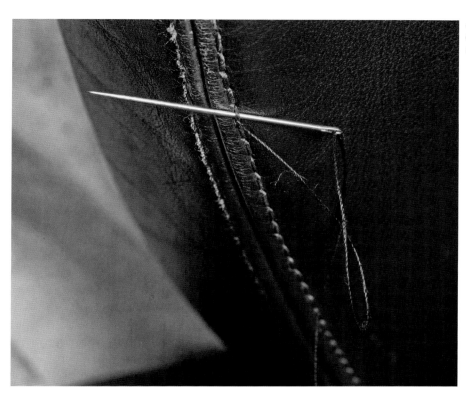

Just as we did at the start, we sewed beyond the opening and into a good, existing seam so that a new opening doesn't form below our repair, later.

As a final touch, we dyed the worn leather (see Project 10) to make the repair as unnoticeable as possible.

PROJECT 16
Replacing a Worn-Out or Broken Seat

 Skill Level: easy/intermediate

 Time Required: 30–45 minutes

 Tools/Supplies Required: seat, wrench

Parts Source: salvage yard

 Cost Estimate: $75–$150 depending on car

If a seat's only failing is the stitched seam, you may be able to sew it as we did in the previous project. When the damage is more extensive, you're often better off replacing the seat with a suitable used item from a wrecking yard or other used parts seller.

This Ford Explorer's driver's seat, which had broken, was replaced with a leather bucket. The passenger seat is not broken, but it's soiled and worn. A local wrecking yard had a replacement for under $100. Prices for salvage items vary widely and you may be able to do better. The website www.car-part.com allows you to search wrecking yards nationwide at one time. If you take that approach, note that shipping costs for large items can add substantially to the purchase price. The seller should be able to quote you a price, shipped, before you buy.

A worn out or broken seat is inconvenient and discouraging, yet it's a problem you can address. If you can't repair the seat, as we did in Project 15, consider swapping in a good, used replacement.

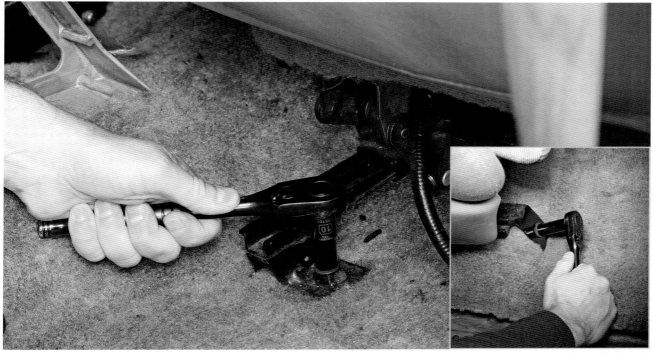

The typical design is for the seat to attach to a track—on which it can move forward and back—which is bolted to the floor. To remove the seat, loosen the bolts securing the track at the front and rear of the seat. If the bolts offer strong resistance, spray a little rust-penetrating lubricant where the bolt head meets the floor and wait—overnight if necessary.

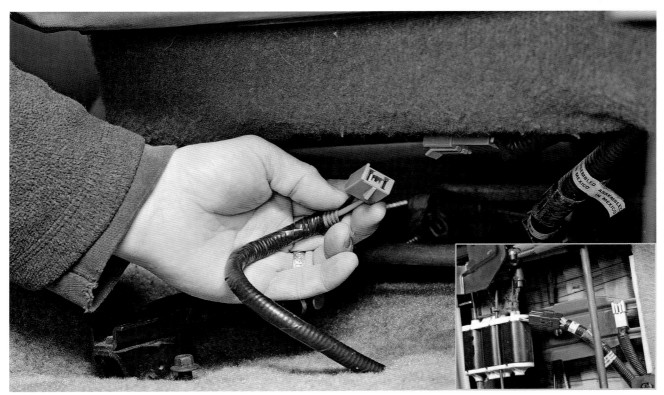

If it's a power seat, there will be an electrical connection between the vehicle's wiring harness and the seat. Find and unplug this connection. As many automotive connectors do, it will likely have a tab that holds the plug together. The slotted tab shown here is attached to the female connector. It slips over and locks behind a tooth on the male end. To undo this connector, you raise the tab as you separate the plug. Many plugs have tabs on both sides; they may require some fiddling to get them free.

Good used seats are easy to come by for popular vehicles. With a little searching, you can find most any style you desire. While the replacement seat is out, you may want to clean and re-grease the tracks for smooth movement. Spray-on white lithium grease works well for this purpose.

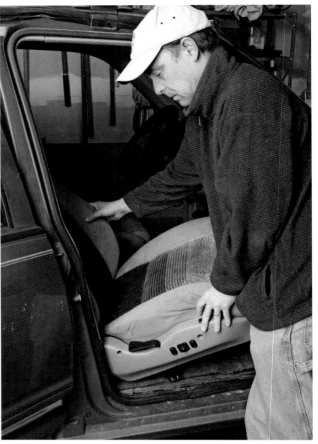

Take care as you pass the seat through the door opening. The metal parts in the track contain sharp edges that will grab at carpet and scratch any paint they rub against. Also keep an eye on the little wiring "pigtail" that connects the car's electrical system to the power seat (if applicable).

Reinstall all mounting bolts and turn them down securely.

Reconnect the power seat plug.

The new fabric seat doesn't match the leather seat on the driver's side, but it is significantly cleaner and more comfortable than the old one!

Repairing a Speaker Grille

 Skill Level: easy to intermediate

 Time Required: 5 to 45 minutes

 Tools/Supplies Required: replacement grille, screwdriver (drill, bits optional)

 Parts Source: auto parts store

 Cost Estimate: varies; this Audi S4 grille cost less than $30

Speaker grilles need to hold their shape—ever see a droopy one? They must also let sound pass through. These two design requirements often produce a honeycomb or mesh face that cannot withstand much force. Put this piece in the path of moving hands or feet and it might get broken.

There are many aftermarket stereo components, including speaker grilles. If you replace only one that is part of a matched pair, you'll want an identical one as the replacement. A dealership may be able to get you one if they are still in production. Otherwise, a salvage yard may have what you need. You can also search online at a website like http://www.car-part.com, which will simultaneously search many salvage yards near you or nationwide.

Placed where the front driver and passenger must swing their foot to exit the vehicle, this speaker grille has been kicked many times, and it eventually cracked.

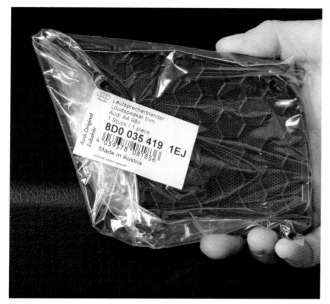

Getting a replacement identical to the broken one was as simple as ordering it from the dealership with this 2001 Audi. They did not have it in stock, but it arrived in two to three days. Some speaker grilles snap into place, held by clips or tabs that may be engaged and released with careful pressure. Other grilles are secured by small screws or bolts. The parts counter at the dealership said that this one popped off. We took a close look at it to confirm this impression and it seemed correct. The four pins off the back side were not threaded inside.

To avoid scratching the surrounding upholstery, we pried up a corner of the old speaker grille with a screwdriver wrapped in masking tape. It withstood a lot of pressure and stayed put. We broke it in pieces getting it out and observed that the pins had been glued into place. That's unusual and was probably something a prior owner did for a speaker grille that wouldn't stay put.

Installing the new piece required removing any pin that broke off and lodged in its mounting hole. One of these was firmly lodged and had to be drilled out.

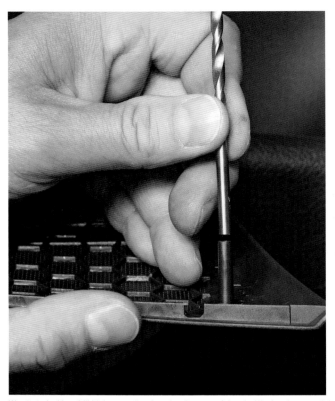

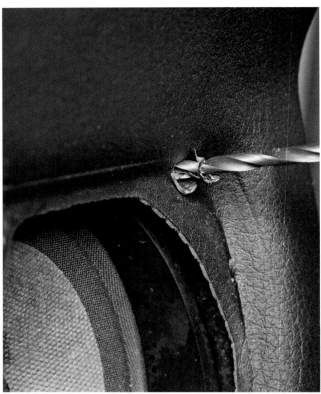

We started with a drill bit just smaller than the diameter of the pin. We then increased the drill bit size by tiny increments.

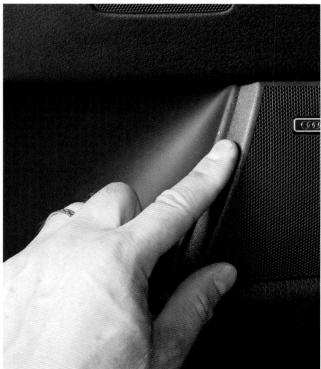

The hole was the correct size when the pins on the speaker grille would press in snugly but not with so much resistance as to risk the pin or grille breaking. The driver will need to keep the new grille in mind when exiting the vehicle so it doesn't get kicked and broken like the original piece.

PROJECT 18
Cleaning a Stained Visor

 Skill Level: easy

 Tools/Supplies Required: upholstery cleaner, rags, brush (optional)

 Time Required: 15 minute

 Parts Source: auto parts store

Cost Estimate: $5–15

Sun visors serve two main purposes: keeping the sun out of your eyes and holding a mirror so you can see whether your hair is combed or you got that grease smudge off your face. They resist or accumulate dirt as well as the rest of the interior and are typically made from the same material. If you damage a visor, you can replace it with one secured from a dealership, a salvage yard, or online.

Cleaning a visor can be accomplished with the same techniques and supplies you would use to clean the seat or dashboard.

This visor has a dirty smudge.

We used a foam upholstery cleaner, but a mild detergent such as laundry detergent dissolved in a bucket would work as well.

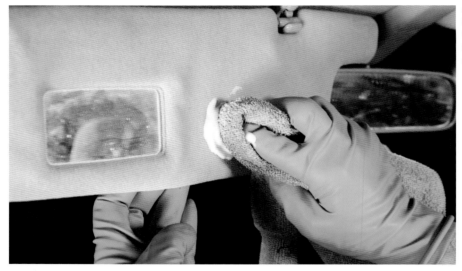

Apply your cleaner or detergent and rub it throughout the area including the stain. If there was a stain, as well as mild dirt distributed over the whole visor, clean it all to avoid a "reverse stain"— an isolated patch of bright, clean material.

If the visor has a mirror, clean that while you're at it, keeping in mind that it could be plastic. If it is, the cleaner for the mirror must be plastic-compatible.

PROJECT 19
Cleaning out and Vacuuming the Interior and Trunk

 Skill Level: easy

 Tools/Supplies Required: shop vac (house vac will do in a pinch

 Time Required: 30 to 60 minutes

 Parts Source: auto parts store

 Cost Estimate: $0

We've included this project because a cluttered, grungy vehicle is hard to deal with. You get in it, get where you're going, and get out, and if there's any cargo that needs to go with you, you stow it quickly somewhere, anywhere, and slam the door. Mess is a challenge for the psyche, not the intellect. But it's a test that feels great to pass. We'll show you the steps and the uplifting results for motivation—and because for vehicles that need it, this work must precede most of the other projects in this book.

Ugh. Much of our reservation in tackling this mess comes from our knowledge that more work is here than meets the eye. Some of this stuff is flat-out junk to be thrown away. Other things will be kept—but not here. So to clean up the car means to sort through it, make decisions, and relocate items to other places with the vaguely menacing prospect of starting another mess elsewhere with what gets moved from this one. The only answer is to proceed. Put the car in good light and open space, get a trash can for the garbage, and be prepared to move other items not going into it.

Here's the same trunk cleaned out. Garbage has been thrown out, what can be recycled has been put into bins for that and the CRT monitor went into an appropriate solid waste facility. Internet sites for your city or county will tell you where to go to dispose of hazardous items.

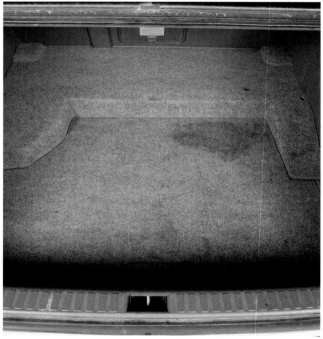

Your shop vac can pull out all the particles that are too small to remove by hand but keep the car looking dirty if they aren't removed. The big hurdle with cleaning out clutter was starting, and once we do, the project rolls to a tidy finish—garbage gone, retained items sorted and put away. (See Projects 21 and 22 regarding that carpet stain.)

Here's a car interior in need of the same treatment.

Remove objects of value and that are too large to vacuum, and then pull up cinders, popcorn, gum wrappers, dirt, and other small debris with your shop vac. If you don't have a shop vac, a home vacuum cleaner will work for dry vacuuming. You can also go to a car wash and use their powerful vacuums and spare yours the wear and tear.

Get the area beside the seats, as well as in front of and behind them. Now that's an interior you can feel good about!

PROJECT 20
Cleaning Floor Mats

 Skill Level: easy

 Tools/Supplies Required: wet/dry shop vac, garden hose (or go to self-serve car wash)

 Time Required: 15 to 30 minutes

 Parts Source: auto parts store

 Cost Estimate: $0–$10

Floor mats last longer—and look better—if you keep them clean. Otherwise the grit that collects there serves as an abrasive to accelerate wear as you move your feet around. A self-serve car wash is a great place to do this job because it will offer both a powerful vacuum cleaner and a high-pressure washer. If that's not convenient or you prefer to work at home, your shop vac and garden hose will work too.

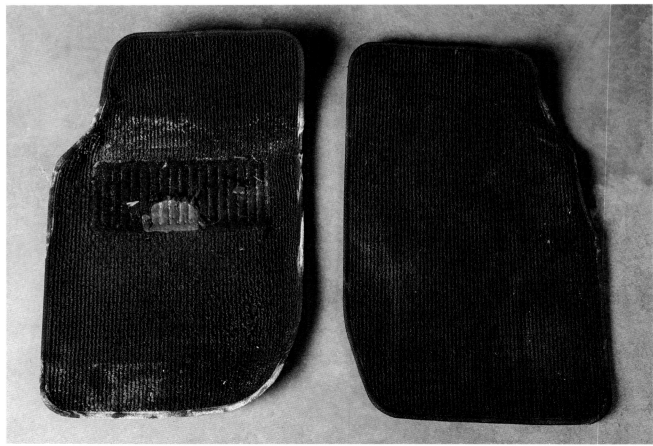

Our floor mats blend with any other dirt, dust, mud, or road salt on the floor of the vehicle. In that setting, the fact that they could benefit from a good cleaning may not be noticeable. Removed and set in bright light on a driveway or concrete slab, their dirty condition is highlighted.

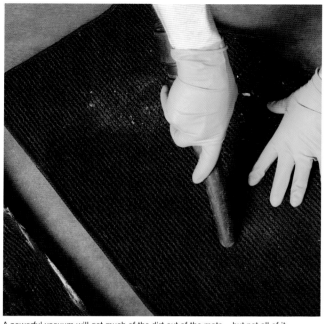

A powerful vacuum will get much of the dirt out of the mats—but not all of it.

The pressure washer at a car wash will get out the rest of the dirt.

Clean the back of the mat, too, to keep as much dirt out of your vehicle as possible.

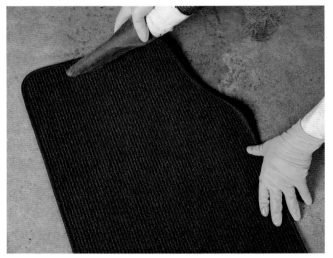

A wet/dry vac will pull out much of the remaining water. To finish drying the mats, set or hang them in a clean spot in the sun.

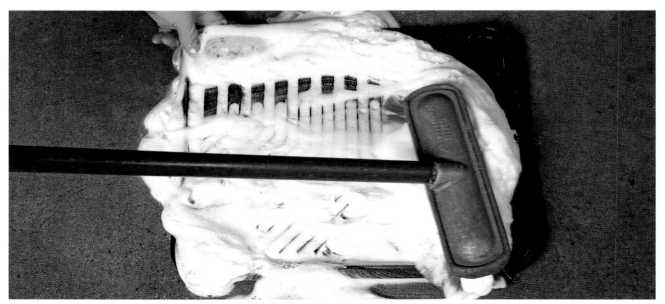

Rubber floor mats clean up well with a car-wash soaping brush. Get both sides here too.

You can use a rag to remove stubborn particles from the mat pattern. Allow the mat to dry before returning it to the vehicle.

PROJECT 21
Shampooing Carpet

 Skill Level: easy

 Time Required: 15 to 45 minutes

 Tools/Supplies Required: carpet/rug cleaner or suds, brush, bucket, wet/dry shop vac

 Parts Source: discount or auto parts store

 Cost Estimate: $0–$15

In the last project, we cleaned up the floor mats. As soon as you remove them, the amount of dirt on the rest of the vehicle's floor will become obvious. Cinders, coins, and trash work their way under the mats and into the carpet, and dirt from our shoes and boots collects on any surface they contact.

When carpet dirt won't vacuum out, a carpet shampoo machine or hand scrubbing with a brush and cleaner will do the trick.

A lot of dirt was hidden under the floor mats in this Volvo. The synthetic fibers used for automotive carpets are highly resistant to staining, however, so we should be able to make them look considerably better.

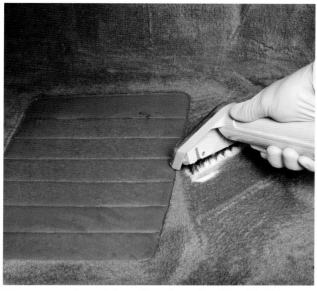

This consumer-grade carpet shampooing system works well for a job of this scope. It incorporates water jets behind the vacuum head, a brush for scrubbing, and a soap-and-water reservoir that delivers suds to the work area.

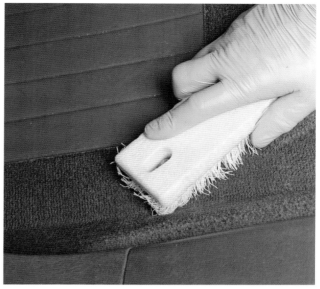

A stiff brush is also helpful for scrubbing out dirt. Use suds during this process too.

Virtually all of the staining came up, leaving the floor in fine shape for its age, suitable for many more years of service.

PROJECT 22
Removing Odors/Freshening the Air

 Skill Level: easy

 Tools/Supplies Required: carpet or upholstery cleaner (depending on location of spill, if any), shop vac, brush

 Time Required: 15 minutes

 Parts Source: discount or auto parts store

 Cost Estimate: $0–$15

One December many years ago, a friend from high school bought a squid at the Italian Market in Philadelphia and hid it under the seat of an upperclassman's Chevy Nova BB. A few weeks later, there was a good thaw and the subject of this prank was out in the student parking lot with the doors and windows open and a none-too-happy face. Years later, the writer of the movie *Grumpy Old Men* put a similar gag into his script—this time with a fish.

How the owners of either of those vehicles got the smell out, I don't know. The method we show you here would be as good as any. First, find the source of the odor and remove it. From there, you may need deodorizer until the final residues of the stinky substance have dissipated.

Toxic chemicals, like heavy-duty solvents and cleaners, are more than stinky. They can make you sick. If you spill chemicals in your car, do not breathe the fumes.

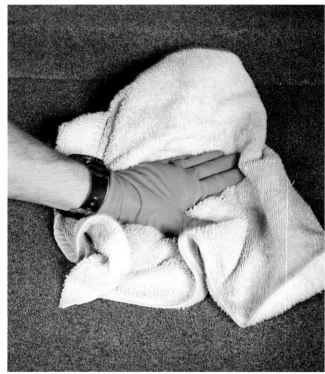

To be rid of a foul smell, you have to remove the source. A stinky liquid got spilled in the trunk of this Volvo. Shampooing the carpet, as we did in Project 21, would be a good approach here. You could also use liquid detergent from a spray-bottle to break down the spill, then scrub the area with a terry cloth rag.

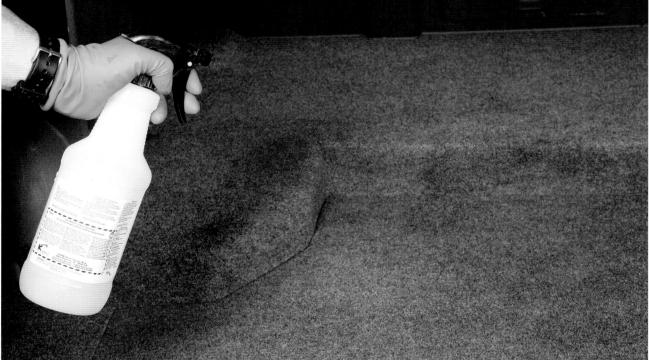

Cleaned and dried with a wet/dry shop vac and towels, we have removed the odor source. Now we treat the area with a professional spray-on deodorizer. Go light with deodorizers to start, as they can produce an aroma of their own. You can always try the old-school deodorizers that hang from the rearview mirror too. They are portable, so if you don't like the scent they produce, you can remove them entirely or shift them farther away inside the vehicle—such as into the hatchback area or trunk.

SECTION 3
BASIC PAINT AND BODY REPAIR

Auto painting is a specialized skill requiring professional spray and safety equipment for large areas and flawless results. There are things anyone can do, however, to make the car's existing finish cleaner and brighter and to repair small scratches to minimize rust. Your work needn't be perfect or show-quality for it to improve the car's looks significantly. Try these projects and you'll see what we mean.

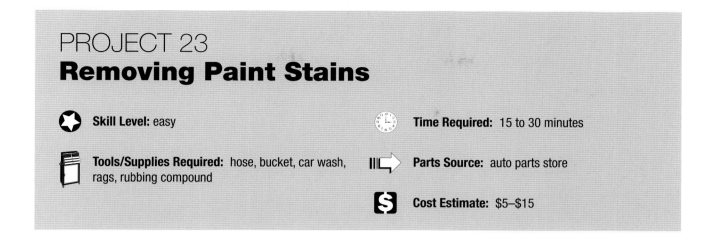

PROJECT 23
Removing Paint Stains

⭐ **Skill Level:** easy

🗄 **Tools/Supplies Required:** hose, bucket, car wash, rags, rubbing compound

🕐 **Time Required:** 15 to 30 minutes

➡ **Parts Source:** auto parts store

💲 **Cost Estimate:** $5–$15

A basic wash and wax will remove most dirt and contaminants that collect on your vehicle's finish. Occasionally a more stubborn stain will be left behind. The less often the car has been washed and waxed beforehand, the harder it will be to get the stain off.

Doing so may require removing some paint—the portion holding the stain. When that's the case, as in this project, we will remove only a fraction of a millimeter in thickness, using polish rather than sandpaper.

If left on for too long, any foreign substance can stain your car's paint.

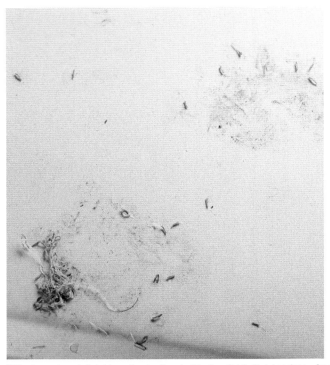

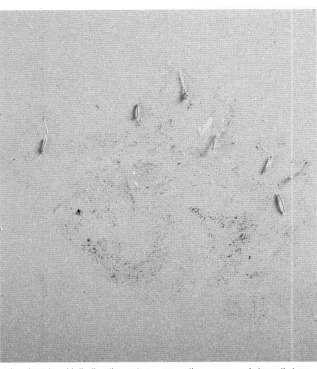

Sitting leaves have left stubborn discolorations in this silver finish. Bird droppings—food broken down by a bird's digestive system—are another common substance that can damage paint. Any reactive substance can hurt your car's finish, and the longer it sits the greater the risk.

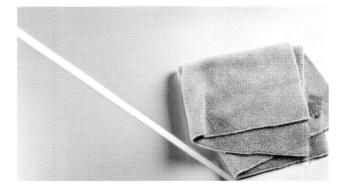

Clean the area with car-wash soap properly mixed with water and rinse well to see how much of the stain remains.

Put polishing, or rubbing, compound onto a soft cloth or pad and rub it throughout the affected area, using a circular motion. You will notice the rag taking on the paint's color as the outer-most layer begins to rub off.

The stain that was here came out completely. You can remove most paint stains this way.

This door has a more stubborn problem: adhesive from a door molding that has come off. Removing this will require a special adhesive or "goo" remover.

If you obtain parts from a wrecking yard, they may be marked with a grease pencil or other semi-permanent marker. It took lacquer thinner, a rag, and some rubbing to get these marks off.

PROJECT 24
Polishing Oxidized Paint

 Skill Level: easy (by hand) to Intermediate (with buffer)

 Tools/Supplies Required: rags, rubbing compound, buffer and buffing pads (optional)

 Time Required: 15 to 60 minutes

 Parts Source: auto parts store

 Cost Estimate: $5–$15

As they do with headlight lenses (Project 3), sunlight and environmental exposure will oxidize paint, leaving a faded, hazy appearance. The once red paint on this Toyota has taken on a whitish hue. There is good paint below it, though, and we can even out the color and restore luster with the same technique we used for the paint stain in the previous project.

Hand or machine buffing will greatly improve the look of oxidized paint. All it takes is rubbing compound and a little elbow grease.

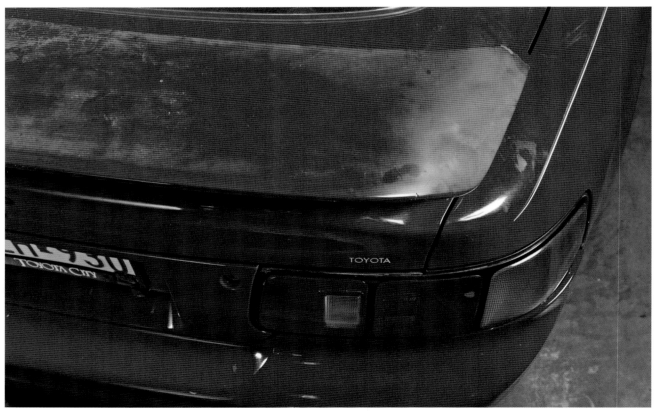

This is the classic oxidized look—hazy, faded, and whitish.

Apply rubbing compound to the oxidized paint. For best results, work on one portion of the faded area at a time.

We polished this by hand with a terry cloth rag and applied firm even pressure in a circular motion. Keep applying rubbing compound and use fresh portions of rag.

As you work the compound into the paint, you will move paint molecules around and some of them will color your rag. That means you're getting the damaged part of the finish off and exposing good paint.

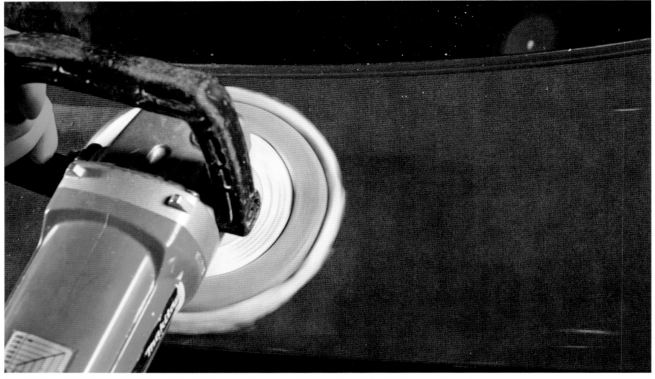

We had access to a power buffer, so we tried it, but the difference was negligible. You can get an excellent result by hand . . .

. . . and here it is.

PROJECT 25
Touching Up a Scratch

 Skill Level: intermediate

 Tools/Supplies Required: rags, degreaser, touch-up paint, artist's brush (optional)

 Time Required: 15 to 45 minutes

 Parts Source: auto parts store

 Cost Estimate: $5–$25 (off-the-shelf paint is cheaper than mixed-to-order)

Unless you live in the desert, a scratch in your car's paint will soon rust. You can head off rust, and make the scratch barely noticeable, with some touch-up paint. Touching up a scratch in this way is an alternative to a professional paint shop's approach of sanding it out, using a skim coat of body filler, sanding that to perfection, then priming and re-painting the finish, blending it into surrounding panels.

The latter method will yield a perfect result, but it requires specialized skills, products, facilities, and safety procedures. Our goal is to minimize the damage and improve your vehicle's appearance while protecting the metal below the touch-up paint. You can do the little jobs yourself; if you need a larger repair, contact a paint shop and see what they can do. There are shops out there that will take on smaller projects and do rust repair, too, at reasonable prices. We've omitted rust repair entirely from this book because the best way to handle rusted metal is to cut it out, weld in fresh steel, and apply the same professional paint techniques described above. For do-it-yourself painting instruction, we recommend another book in the Motorbooks Workshop series, *How to Paint Your Car* by Dennis W. Parks and David H. Jacobs.

You can get touch-up paint from various sources. Auto parts shops have bottles on the shelf of the most popular colors. Some of them—check the yellow pages or Internet—can also mix paint if you bring them the color code. Your owner's manual will tell you where to find this; it's typically on a sticker in the door frame or in the trunk or hatchback area. For the small areas we'll do here, we will use brush-on rather than spray-on paint. Any time you spray, you will cover a much larger area and will need to mask off anything that you don't want to get painted.

If the scratch on your car has gone all the way through the color coat and the primer and exposed bare metal, follow the procedures here with auto body primer first and then with color. You can buy brush-on primer, or, if you get it in a spray can, shake well, spray some into the can's plastic lid, and dip your brush there to get a small amount to paint into the scratch. If light rust has formed in the scratch, use a mildly abrasive sandpaper, like 400, folded so as to stay confined to the scratch area, and sand off the rust, then clean out the scratch with degreaser before priming and painting.

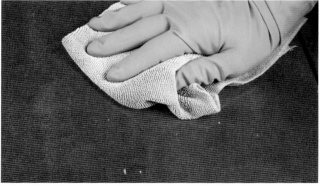 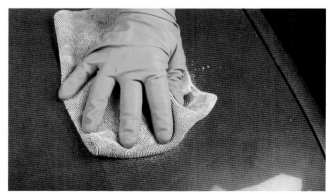

Before painting, clean the scratches you plan to touch up with alcohol or, as we did here, a spray-on degreaser. In a pinch, glass cleaner will work. You want something that removes contaminants, dries fast, and leaves no residue.

Find a comfortable body position to address the scratch—ideally, one where you can set part of your arm on the vehicle for support as you paint.

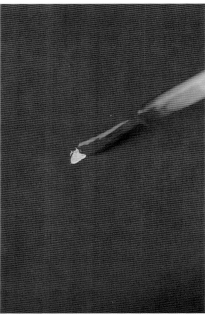

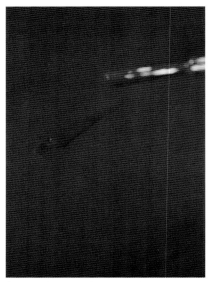

With a small amount of paint on the brush, set it in the scratch and paint the length of it in one motion, lifting the brush away at the end of the scratch. Allow the touched-up area to dry and avoid touching it or washing the car for the period recommended by the manufacturer in the product directions.

Touch-up paint bottles feature a brush attached to the cap. However, you may prefer to use an artist's brush, which will allow you to make a finer line. After you dip either brush in the paint, wipe most of it off on the lip of the bottle, because the brush will hold more paint than you think.

PROJECT 26
Popping Out a Small Dent

 Skill Level: intermediate

 Tools/Supplies Required: screwdriver, wrench, tape, razorblade

 Time Required: 45 minutes to 1.5 hours

 Parts Source: auto parts store

 Cost Estimate: $0

Heavy collision damage is beyond the scope of our book. Yet a small dent is something the average vehicle owner can pop out. How visible the dent will be afterwards depends on the extent of the damage and how well you approach it. You will get the best result if you can get at the back side of the point of impact. Pushing there will help you reverse what happened initially. To get at the back of the dent, you will likely have to remove some interior panels.

If there is a dent but no paint damage, as can happen from hail or a tap from a modern plastic-capped bumper, paintless dent repair (PDR) is an alternative to popping it yourself. Also, if you pop it yourself and the result isn't as attractive as you'd like, you may need to bring your car to a PDR specialist.

This door got bumped in a parking garage. The paint is not damaged but the sheet metal is pushed in where a ridge runs through the door.

We need access to the back side of the door to pop out the dent. To get that access, we will remove the interior door panel.

This vehicle has a window crank and door lock that connect through the panel to hardware on the back side. We need to remove them. The door lock unscrews and this window crank comes free when you pop out the trim ring below. (See Project 36 for additional photos on crank handles.)

The anchoring screws for this VW Golf's interior door panel are behind the grab handle, which pops off with a small screwdriver.

Any speaker mounted to the door panel itself will need to be unplugged from the car's wiring harness. (The extended finger here is for support; it is not pointing out anything.) On this vehicle the door handle stays with the door. Some door designs may require that your remove the handle or surrounding parts to free the door panel.

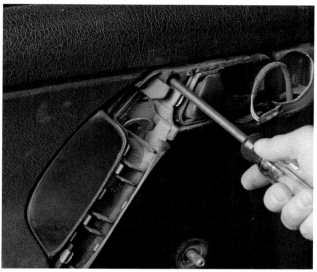

When you have access to the door panel's mounting bolts or screws, remove them with the appropriate screwdriver or wrench.

Door panels mount through a combination of bolts (or screws) and clips. This particular one uses plastic clips to which the panel is secured with small bolts. If the clips would pull free, we would not need to undo the bolts. They held securely, however, under as much force as we were comfortable applying—we did not want to break them. So, we unbolted the panel and left the plastic clips snapped into their mounting holes in the door.

The plastic cover over the main speaker came off when we unbolted the clips, but the main panel and the speaker stayed put, indicating that the speaker bolts were also panel fasteners. (The tweeter came off with the door handle after we unplugged it.) We unscrewed the speaker and removed it and the main door panel.

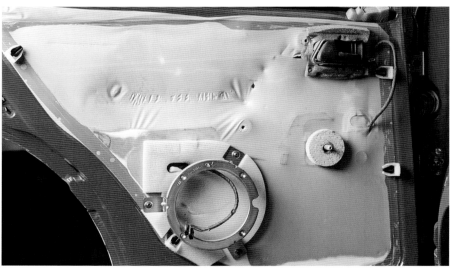

The plastic sheet is a moisture barrier that prevents water entering the car after running down the window and into the door. That water drains through one or more holes in the bottom of the door. (If they get plugged, collected water will cause rust. Check them once in a while and clear them with a small nail, paper clip, etc., as necessary.) We slit the barrier with a razorblade and lifted it out of the way, exposing the back of the dent.

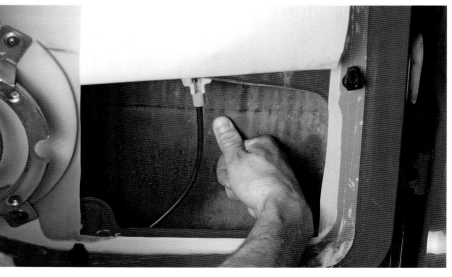

Our pop-out tool is a thumb (because it has no sharp edges). We tried to push in the deepest part of the dent. Pushing on this spot caused the dent to pop out.

The majority of the dent came out. Depending on light and view angle, it's no longer noticeable. If you wanted to make it perfect, a paintless dent repair shop could likely do that for you. From this point, we used plastic tape to restore the moisture barrier and put back the parts removed previously. Keeping all your fasteners organized as you remove them helps you get all of them back onto the vehicle in the right place.

PROJECT 27
Replacing a Fender

 Skill Level: intermediate

 Tools/Supplies Required: replacement fender

 Time Required: about 2 hours

 Parts Source: salvage yard

 Cost Estimate: $50–$100

Rust and collisions can ruin a fender (or other body panel) on an otherwise nice-looking vehicle. For common models, replacements are available. Purchased from a dealership or aftermarket supplier, the panel will usually come finished in primer. If you buy one from a salvage yard, however, you may be able to get it with the same paint color as your vehicle. Assuming it's in good condition—confirm this with the yard—you can swap it without repainting, saving effort and money.

That's the approach we took here. We contacted several salvage yards via the Internet and asked about listed fenders of appropriate age and color. When we found one in great shape, and red as needed, we bought it and the yard shipped it. If you find a good one at a yard nearby, you can look at it before you buy.

The driver's side fender on this VW is rough, with a large rust hole behind the wheel and more rust creeping along the wheel opening.

 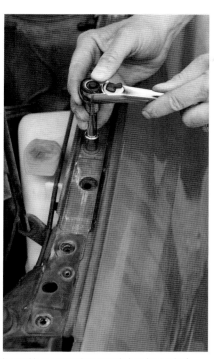 

A line of bolts secure the panel along the top edge. Unbolt these with an appropriate wrench, keeping track of where each one goes, because size may vary.

Plastic fasteners secure a wheelwell liner to the fender.

One way to pry these fasteners loose is with a side cutter. Don't squeeze the handles together more than necessary to stay under the fastener. If the liner slips over the fastener's head, you can pull out the fastener with pliers. Fasteners like these often get damaged on removal. They are common and can be replaced through a dealership or auto parts store.

This liner also had small bolts holding it to the fender. We removed these with a socket wrench (you could use an adjustable, box end, or open end wrench too). When all the anchoring bolts are removed, you can lift off the fender.

The fender liner had a plastic reservoir attached to it, which we left in place. This fender also held the radio antenna. (See Project 38 for more on replacing an antenna.)

Our wrecking yard fender matches the paint on the car. It's a little faded and has an unneeded pinstripe, but the metal is in great shape. No rust holes here.

When you bolt the replacement fender to the car, leave the bolts loose until you get it adjusted to your liking. Check the gaps between the fender and the adjacent panels. For aesthetics, you want these to be even along their length and comparable to the same gap on the other side of the vehicle. Don't make the gap along the leading door edge too narrow. If you do, the door will hit it upon opening and bend something. Open the door slowly the first time to make sure it clears the replacement panel.

Here's the same fender after we removed the pinstripe and wrecking yard marks. We also polished the paint on the fender and the rest of the car, removing oxidation and bringing out the color. (See Projects 7 and 24 for details.)

PROJECT 28
Reapplying Door Molding, Adhesive Type

 Skill Level: intermediate

 Tools/Supplies Required: original door molding, adhesive tape, masking tape, rags, adhesive remover, plastic scraper

 Time Required: 30 minutes to 1 hour

 Parts Source: auto parts store

 Cost Estimate: $10–$25

Door moldings do double duty, adding some design flair—especially on a slab-sided vehicle—and stopping carelessly opened doors on neighboring vehicles from causing a ding, scratch, or both. In time, however, moldings secured by adhesive strips may start to sag, peel away, or fall off.

Fortunately, the same manufacturers who supply adhesive to the automobile industry also offer products in the aftermarket. Double-faced foam adhesive tape will put that missing molding right back where it belongs to give you more years of style and protection.

Typically, the old adhesive leaves residue showing how the manufacturer had the piece attached. We'll follow Dodge's lead with this pickup's door and reattach the molding with three adhesive strips.

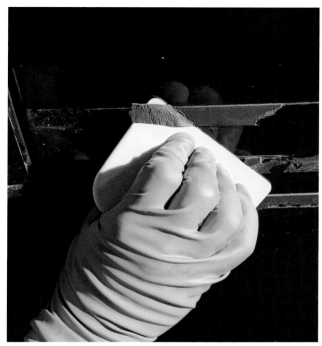

Removing the old adhesive is a two-part process. First, you remove the bulky foam backing. We used a bodywork spatula—available at auto parts stores—to avoid scratching the paint.

Second, remove the adhesive residue. For this, use a citrus or chemical adhesive remover, wearing gloves to protect your skin. This was a tough adhesive that took about 10 minutes to remove—hire a strong neighbor kid if your arm gets tired.

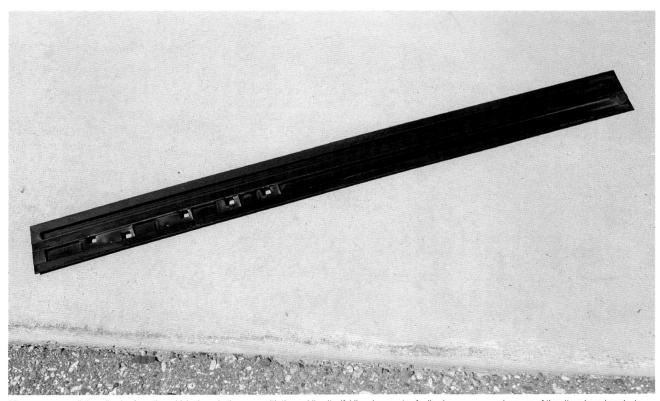

After you remove all the adhesive from the vehicle door, do the same with the molding itself. Liberal amounts of adhesive remover, such as one of the citrus-based products, may be necessary. Make sure the molding is clean, dry, and free of residue.

The manufacturer used three strips of adhesive, so we did too. Peel the backing off one side, stick it along the length of the molding, and trim it at the end.

The trickiest part of this job is getting the molding straight when you reattach it. You'll match it up with the corresponding piece on the adjacent panel, but it will still want to sag because it's heavy rubber. If you don't trust your ability to "eyeball" it, put some automotive masking tape in a straight line just above where you will reattach it and follow that line as you press the molding on from one end to the other. Consider having a helper hold one end of the molding while you carefully reattach from the other.

PROJECT 29
Reattaching Clip-On Molding

⭐ **Skill Level:** easy

🧰 **Tools/Supplies Required:** rags, car-wash soap and water, bucket, molding clips, screwdriver

🕐 **Time Required:** 15 to 30 minutes

▌⇨ **Parts Source:** auto parts store

💲 **Cost Estimate:** $5–$15

In the previous project, we reattached a molding secured with adhesive foam tape. Some moldings are still held in by the old method—clips. When one of these comes loose, it's because a clip has either popped out or broken.

On our demonstration car, the clip pulled free when the door opened against a chainlink fence. The driver shut the door as usual, and the fence hooked the trim strip and pulled it part way off, breaking a few clips. Auto parts stores carry some clips of this type, but we did not find ones identical to the existing clips, so we ordered the needed number of replacement clips from the dealership.

This Volvo's molding clips on via plastic buttons that press into holes in the sheet metal.

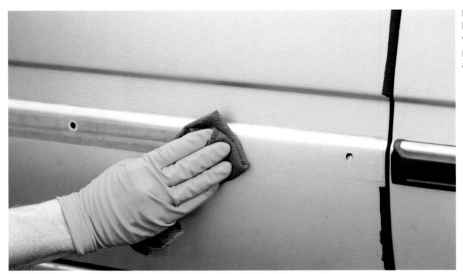

Before reattaching the molding, clean the area below it to get contaminants off the paint. This won't affect the clips' adhesion, but it's good for the paint to remove substances that could scratch it or accelerate rust. (See Project 23.)

We used a screwdriver to pop out the broken clips. Support the molding and be careful to avoid damaging it or hitting your other hand with the screwdriver. Here, we're rotating the screwdriver to produce upward force, not pushing it toward the left hand.

This type of clip features a tapered button with a flared base that clips into the door and a beveled base that snaps into a groove in the molding.

We used the blade of the screwdriver to press the clip's beveled edge downward until it snapped into the molding.

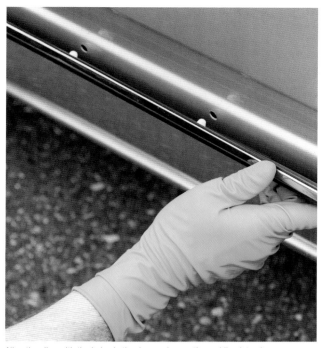

Align the clips with the holes in the door and press the molding into place.

No worries with a clip-on molding being straight. The clips ensure it, if you have all of them.

PROJECT 30
Attaching or Reattaching Mud Flaps

 **Skill Level:** easy

 Tools/Supplies Required: wrench or screwdriver, mud flap

 Time Required: 15 to 45 minutes

 Parts Source: auto parts store

 Cost Estimate: $0–$50

Like side moldings, mud flaps have both a practical and an aesthetic function. They add a little something to the vehicle's looks and keep dirt, salt, and anything else on the road from collecting in quantity behind the wheelwells.

You might add mud flaps to a vehicle that does not have them or replace one that falls off. If the cause of the latter situation was rust, you may need to replace the panel too. (See Project 27.)

On a panel that angles inward like this one, a mud flap will stop dirt and debris that would otherwise be thrown directly onto the vehicle.

BASIC PAINT AND BODY REPAIR

The typical modern mud flap is a molded piece of plastic. Like most other parts, you can find it at a wrecking yard, online, or through a dealership (with availability decreasing for rarer and older models).

If a salvage yard tells you it's a good part, and it doesn't show a lot of cosmetic damage, it should clean up well. This is the same mud flap washed clean.

Fenders and quarter panels of vehicles commonly fitted with mud flaps should be drilled and tapped for them. Otherwise, you can take a drill bit just a tiny amount smaller than the mounting screw, hold the mud flap in place, mark the fender through the hole with a felt-tip marker, and drill. These fasteners were accessible without removing the wheel, but sometimes you need to do so. Up front, you can often turn the steering wheel one way or the other to get the tire out of your way.

This photo shows how much of the body panel the mud flap protects from kicked up mud, salt, and debris—a lot of it.

SECTION 4
GLASS AND MIRRORS

You can and probably do clean the windows and mirrors when you wash your car. However, they're critical to your vision and safety at the wheel and often require cleaning more often than you make time to clean the whole vehicle. Windshields chip, too, and mirrors break. Try these projects to keep a clear and unobstructed view of the road, other drivers, pedestrians, cyclists, and the beautiful world outside.

PROJECT 31
Fixing a Glass Chip

 Skill Level: intermediate

 Tools/Supplies Required: rags, glass cleaner, scissors, glass repair kit

 Time Required: 30 minutes to 1 hour

 Parts Source: auto parts store

 Cost Estimate: $10–$20

Major cracks will doom your windshield, but chips are a mere annoyance. Kits available at your local auto parts store can make chips easier to see through and help prevent them from expanding across your field of vision. (Cracks do expand, from temperature changes and flexing of the vehicle chassis.)

Several manufacturers make kits, and the exact manner of use differs depending on kit components. The basic idea is the same, however; refer to your kit's instructions if it doesn't look like this one. Our effort did not quite produce an undetectable fix—but it does look better and should not crack further. It will also be less distracting in the driver's field of vision.

GLASS AND MIRRORS

This "bull's-eye" chip has a large semicircular crack and two small, straight cracks radiating from the point of impact. Pick any impurities out of the chip with a pin and then clean the glass around the chip, inside and outside, with alcohol or glass cleaner.

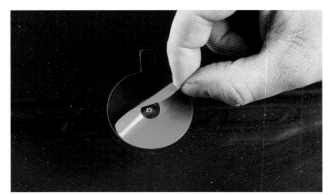

Put the car in a shady spot to keep the windshield from getting too hot from the sun. The kit adheres to the windshield beginning with a double-sided patch, which we will center over the chip. Press it on firmly, ensuring (by looking from the passenger compartment) that there are no air bubbles beneath it.

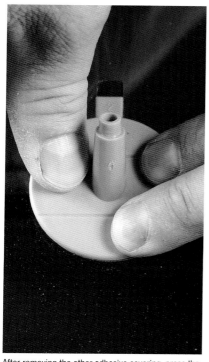

After removing the other adhesive covering, press the plastic base onto the adhesive patch.

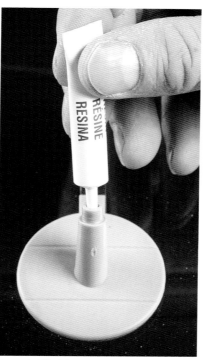

Pour resin (3/4 of the tube, with this kit) into the base, then fit a syringe, fully depressed, over it.

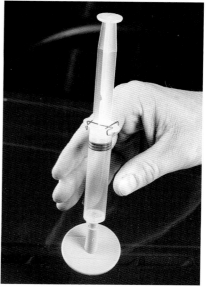

Drawing back and locking the syringe with a little clip creates a vacuum in the chip's airspaces. You then break the vacuum, as we are about to do here, allowing air to enter the plastic base above the resin. Press the syringe inward; this one locks in place, so the resin can fill in the chip. (Follow your kit's specific instructions for how long to wait between steps.)

Use a single-edge razor to break the adhesive's seal and remove the plastic base. Move the car into direct sunlight and place one drop of remaining adhesive on the chip. Set the yellow plastic cover onto the resin and press out the air.

After the prescribed time—15 minutes with our kit—remove the yellow covering. Our repair left part of the crescent-shaped mark, but filled in and eliminated the straight cracks radiating out of the chip. This chip should never grow from this size. The remaining resin will have a faint border, which we left. You can scrape this back with a razorblade, but avoid scraping over the chip itself.

PROJECT 32
Replacing a Side Mirror

 Skill Level: intermediate

 Tools/Supplies Required: screwdriver, socket wrench, replacement mirror

 Time Required: 30 minutes to 1.5 hours

 Parts Source: auto parts store

Cost Estimate: $25–$100

Sideview mirrors protrude many inches from the side of the vehicle. While this allows a good look at cars beside and behind us, it creates opportunity for the sideview mirror to hit something, like a mailbox or some fixture at a gas pump, toll stop, or drive-through window. Such a bump may crack the housing, the mirror glass, or both parts.

On older cars, the mounting screws for a sideview mirror were obvious—sitting in plain view at the base of the mirror. Modern mirrors are attached from within by hidden fasteners that typically require some disassembly of interior trim. There may also be wires or linkage connecting the mirror to a power or mechanical adjustment control.

When the mirror is cracked, it is usually easier to replace the whole mirror assembly than to try to swap out just the glass. Salvage yards are an excellent place to find a good replacement. If the mirror on the opposite side of the vehicle is flawless, you can probably source a new replacement for the damaged side online or from a dealership for an equivalent look.

This is a power mirror, controlled by a small "joystick" that looks a lot like the locking mechanism on older cars. There are two bolts securing the trim panel, along with push-in clips along the back side of the panel perimeter that we cannot see.

Remove attachment screws or bolts with the appropriate wrench or screwdriver. Keep track of what goes where because the lengths may not be the same. On this vehicle, the bottom bolt is longer.

In addition to screws or bolts, interior panels are typically secured by clips that pull off and press on. Pull on these carefully to avoid breaking anything. If you break a clip, you can sometimes replace it; if you crack the panel, that's a more expensive fix. We wrapped the tip of a flat-blade screwdriver with masking tape so we could get behind this panel without scratching the paint. Once you make a gap, pull with your fingers, too, so you can apply force in more than one spot, distributing it to reduce the risk of breaking the panel.

Here is what this manufacturer's concealed clips look like, along with the slot into which they anchor. Pulling back the top portion of the panel revealed the mirror's anchoring bolts and a connection for the power controls. Use something blunt, like a roll of tape or a block of wood to hold the panel out so you can undo these connections.

If you have a power mirror, disconnect the wire connector. You may have to release a locking tab—which we're pulling back with a fingernail here—to separate the connection.

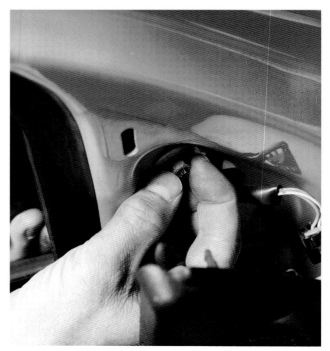

Loosen each bolt or nut and remove them while holding the mirror so that it does not drop and leave broken glass in your work area.

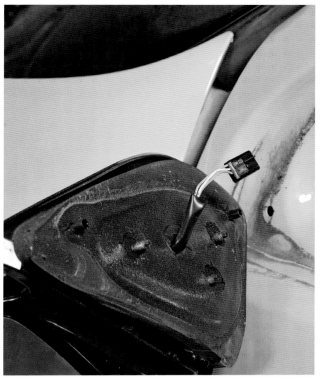

Remove the old mirror, letting the wiring pass through the appropriate hole.

If part of the wiring connection is secured by a tab, slip that over the bolt on the replacement mirror before tightening the nuts. Then reconnect the wiring and tighten up all of the mirror's mounting hardware. Press the trim panel back into place . . .

. . . and the sideview mirror problem is fixed!

PROJECT 33
Reattaching a Rearview Mirror

 Skill Level: intermediate

 Time Required: 15 to 45 minutes

Tools/Supplies Required: rearview mirror epoxy kit, rag, glass cleaner, masking tape, razorblade

 Parts Source: auto parts store

 Cost Estimate: $5–$15

The trend with modern rearview mirrors is to attach them to the windshield glass. The manufacturer applies a powerful adhesive to the back of a small metal plate, which sticks to the glass. The base of the mirror slips over the plate, whose sides are angled and beveled to hold it in place. If the mirror has electronic features, like auto dimming or built-in displays, these are attached to the vehicle's wiring harness by a wire that emerges near the top of the windshield and plugs into the back of the mirror.

Temperature changes, including intense heat, can weaken the glue, allowing the attachment plate to come free. Even with manufacturers who have excellent adhesives from the factory, mirror adhesion can become an issue when the windshield is replaced and the mirror reattached by someone else. Auto parts stores offer a mirror kit with the correct glue to put the mirror back where it belongs.

This patch of adhesive is all that remains after this vehicle's rearview mirror let loose.

Before you remove the old glue, mark the attachment point with masking tape from the outside. That way, once the glue is gone and the glass cleaned, you can still find the best place to position the mirror.

With the mirror location marked by tape, use a single-edge razorblade to clean up any old adhesive. We'll be wearing gloves later in this project when we work with the new adhesive. At this point, you may find it easier to hold and control the razorblade without them. Do whatever you're most comfortable with and always use extreme care when working with a sharp tool of any kind.

When you're done with the razorblade, put the cardboard blade cover back over the blade and set it in your toolbox so it won't cut you or your upholstery. Now spray glass cleaner in the mirror-mounting area and clean it with a rag. The area needs to be clean to ensure good adhesion with the new glue.

For solid attachment, you'll want the back of the mounting plate to be free of old glue.

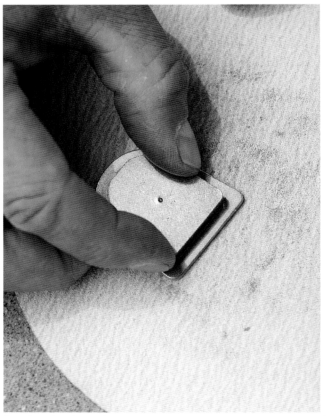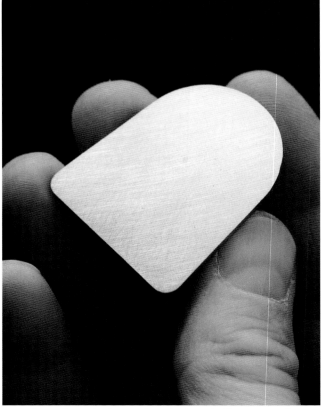

Set a piece of sandpaper of about 180 to 200 grit on a flat surface, like your garage or basement floor, and move the plate over it in a circular motion. This will clean off the old glue and leave you with a clean, slightly porous surface for the new adhesive.

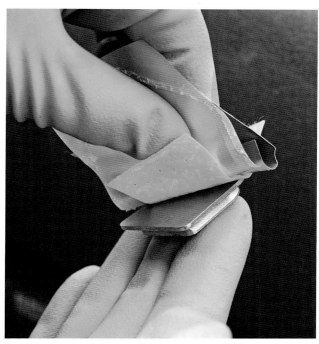

If you haven't had gloves on up to this point, put them on now. Our kit uses a two-stage adhesive. The first stage utilizes a swab concealed in a foil envelope. You open the envelope, peel it backwards and swab both the attachment point on the windshield and the back of the metal plate.

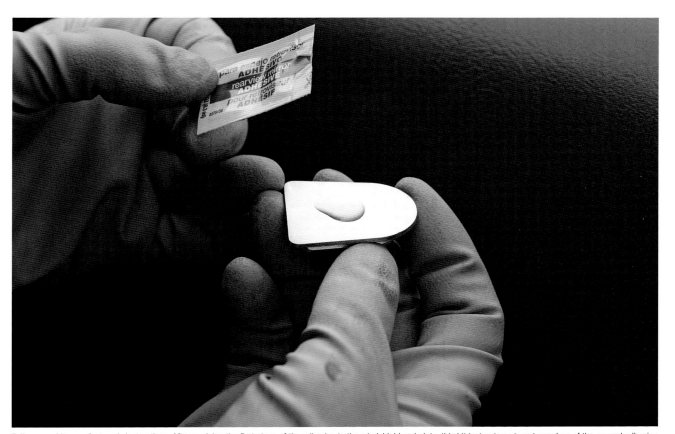

Follow your kit manufacturer's instructions. After applying the first stage of the adhesive to the windshield and plate, this kit instructs us to put one drop of the second adhesive onto the plate.

Press it onto the interior glass at the tape mark. Our kit said to hold it for one minute, then allow 15 minutes before hanging the mirror on it.

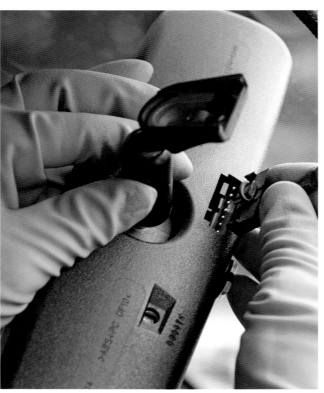

This mirror had electronics that we connect with a plug in the back of the mirror. The final step with this style mirror was to reinstall a set screw that prevents the mirror from wobbling on the base plate. Remove the masking tape and the job is done.

PROJECT 34
Repairing Plastic-Coated Window Trim

 Skill Level: intermediate

Tools/Supplies Required: razorblade masking tape, paint

 Time Required: 30 minutes to 1 hour

 Parts Source: auto parts store

 Cost Estimate: $10–$15

Some vehicles have black trim around the window exterior. When this trim is a plastic coating sprayed on aluminum, it can shrink and crack. An easy and attractive way to repair this common problem is to strip off the coating with a razorblade and re-coat the surface with a thick spray paint.

The once attractive black trim below this window has been reduced by the elements to a ragged flap of peeled-off coating.

GLASS AND MIRRORS

109

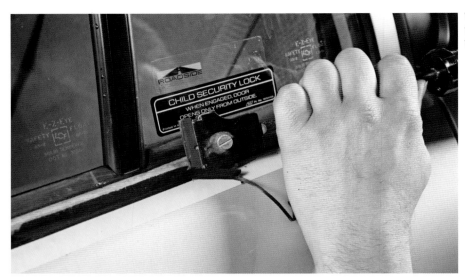

We're going to scrape off the old coating, but first we'll run a line of masking tape beneath it to protect the paint as we work.

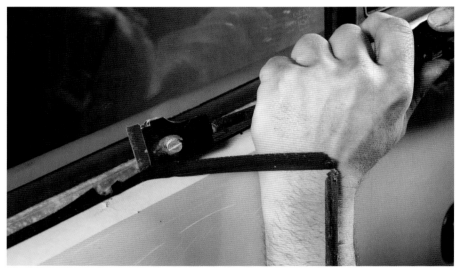

This scraper is nothing more than a single-edge razorblade in a handle. The handles are available at auto parts and hardware stores and provide good control over the sharp blade. Be careful not to cut through the rubber strip that presses against the bottom edge of the window glass.

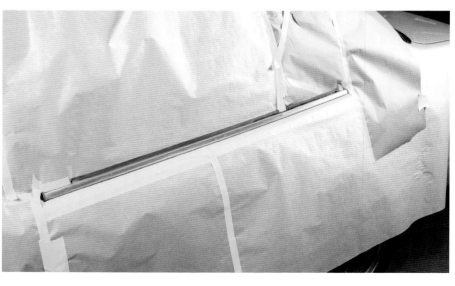

Once all of the old trim coating has been scraped away, we mask off the glass and surrounding metal with masking tape and paper so that nothing except the trim strip gets hit by spray paint.

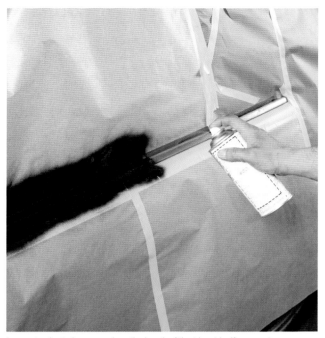

In one steady stroke, spray along the length of the trim strip. If you want a long-lasting repair, spray a coat of primer and allow it to dry before you spray satin black paint. You want to paint slowly enough that the paint lays on shiny, rather than light and dusty looking, but not so slowly that runs develop. If you haven't painted much, find a junk piece of metal, like a can, and use it to test your technique until you get it right.

Remove the masking tape and paper before the paint has dried. This approach prevents the masking tape from pulling dried paint off your finished surface. If any paint got behind your masking tape, wipe it off with a rag dipped in lacquer thinner—wear rubber gloves for that operation, folding the rag to give you a fine tip.

Much better! This is more like the window looked when the car was new.

SECTION 5
CONVENIENCE AND COSMETIC REPAIRS

Here are a few more projects you may encounter as you continue to haul people and goods with your trusty transportation. We recommend that you purchase a good repair manual for your year, make, and model vehicle to supplement the knowledge you gain here. By now you've gained the confidence to tackle a variety of repairs. If a problem can be fixed by anyone with the skills, know-how, and inclination, that person could be you. You can do it!

PROJECT 35
Replacing a Topper Strut

Skill Level: easy

Tools/Supplies Required: screwdriver, replacement struts

Time Required: 15 to 30 minutes

Parts Source: auto parts store

Cost Estimate: $30–$60

Gas-filled struts appear on cars and trucks as supports to hold up panels like the hood or trunk, or the rear window on a topper. The strut lengthens slowly as you open the desired panel and then supports it until you compress the gas in the strut by pushing the panel closed and latching it.

In this project, we replaced the struts supporting the rear window in a truck topper. A similar technique applies to struts on hoods and trunks too. Check the pressure rating, in pounds per square inch (psi) of your old strut as you purchase the new one(s). Too much or too little pressure and the replacement will not work well.

Tailgates, hoods, and hatchbacks often utilize gas-filled struts for support when open. When the seals go, the strut no longer does its job.

The typical attachment for a strut like this uses a spring-steel clip that fits over a ball joint. Put a screwdriver behind the clip and pry to pull the clip's ends off of the ball joint.

The end of the strut pivots on a ball joint.

As you can see, the clip makes the cavity in the strut too small for the ball on the ball joint to slip out.

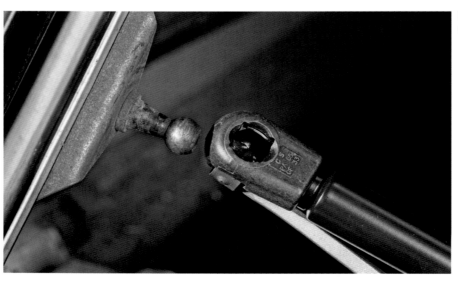

With this style strut, you can retract the clip with a screwdriver.

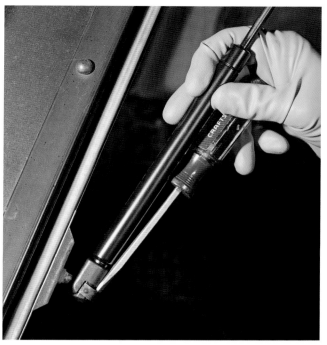 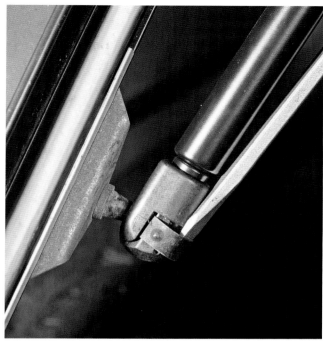

Holding the clip out allows easy installation or removal. Lever the clip out only far enough to remove the strut—you don't want to pop the clip out of the end of the strut.

The new strut, like the old, attaches to ball joints on the window and topper.

PROJECT 36
Replacing a Window Crank

 Skill Level: easy to intermediate

 Tools/Supplies Required: small screwdriver, replacement crank

 Time Required: 15 to 45 minutes

Parts Source: auto parts store

 Cost Estimate: $10–$25

Roll-up, or manual, windows are less common on today's vehicles, but they are convenient in the precise control they provide—unlike most power windows, which seem eager to glide all the way down (especially in a downpour). But a window crank handle can wear out, fall off, break, or become wobbly. In such case, you may want to replace it.

On classic vehicles, the knob may be attached by a screw visible at the base of the crank. More recent models tend to hide the connection. You may imagine that it's just a press-fit in that case and that you can pop the handle off if you pull hard enough. Odds are, that is not the case and you will break the handle or the securing mechanism.

Recent crank handles commonly utilize a groove in the shaft protruding through the door. A clip or pin passes through the back of the handle, locking it in place. We'll walk you through the process for replacing them.

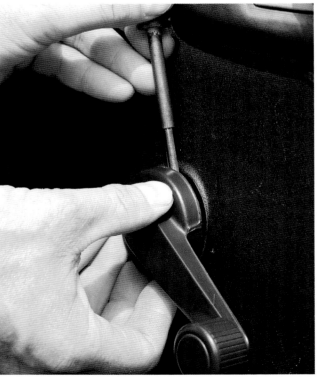

This Chevrolet window crank handle secures with a clip passing through grooves on the back side. To see it, press a screwdriver between the back of the handle and the washer protecting the door trim from the mechanism. The washer may be made of plastic.

For perspective, here is the window crank shaft with its groove, the clip that passes through both the handle and the shaft, and the washer protecting the door trim.

The clip passes through slots in the handle and fits into the groove on the shaft. To remove the handle, you need to pop off this clip with a screwdriver or other small tool. On this handle, the clip can point either direction. You'll need to figure out which way it points to remove it.

Attaching the replacement handle involves positioning the clip on the handle, pushing the handle onto the crank shaft far enough to align the clip and the groove, and popping the clip down so it locks in the groove. Point the clip whichever way is easiest for you to reach and push (i.e., toward or away from the handle).

This VW Golf uses the same basic approach of grooved shaft on the door and clip passing through the crank handle. The trick here is to pull out the ring on the base of the handle—directly away from the knob—using a small screwdriver. The reverse-side shot, with the base ring still displaced for removal, shows how the white clips will snap into the groove once you reinstall the handle and shift the base ring back toward the crank knob.

PROJECT 37
Recharging the Air Conditioning System

 Skill Level: easy

 Tools/Supplies Required: A/C recharge kit

Time Required: 15 to 30 minutes

 Parts Source: auto parts store

 Cost Estimate: $25–$35

The age when air conditioning (A/C) in an automobile was a novel luxury are long past. A/C is commonplace on our cars and a veritable necessity for people in hot climates who need or want to look good—that is, to not have a windblown hairdo at their destination. And sometimes, e.g., when it's hot and raining, the window is a lousy option.

Air conditioning systems are pressurized, and as the years pass, the refrigerant often manages to find its way to equilibrium by escaping through the most microscopic breach. Dealerships and garages can recharge your system for a three-figure sum. Or, you can do it yourself quickly and for a fraction of that cost with a simple recharge kit available at auto parts stores and online.

Wear gloves for this procedure—and eyeglasses or safety glasses too. You're dealing with extreme cold and high pressure, so it's important to protect your eyes and skin. The approach for this kit is typical. Read the information provided with the kit you purchase and follow their directions exactly for your best result.

The standard refrigerant for newer vehicles is called R-134a, and many vehicles that predate the cutoff point (1995) have been retrofitted to use it. The older system is R12. If your vehicle was built for that and has not been converted, do not use the R-134a kit.

This early-1990s engine has been converted to the new refrigerant. Our recharge kit has a hose that will fit here, to the low-pressure fitting leading into the compressor. (The high-pressure side of the compressor—the side into which the compressor is pumping—has a different-size fitting that will not connect to the kit's hose.)

Turn the valve clockwise so that it punctures the top of the coolant can, then slowly turn it back until a little coolant escapes and purges the hose of air. Close the valve again and attach the hose to the low-pressure fitting on your A/C system.

ective cap. The low-pressure service port is located between the evaporator and the compressor
under the dash or in the engine compartment close to the firewall.

position, shake can well and screw can onto recharge hose. Keep gauge in up postion and proceed.
ndle clockwise until the piercing stem is completely in the down position and proceed. Checking
to escape.

ompressor clutch is engaged and
f the compressor still does not engage,

connector ring back as you push the
the can of refrigerant may burst,

with these instructions. Ambient
outside of the vehicle. Add
struction #4 below. When charging
low.

Ambient Temp (°F)	Low Side Gauge
65°	25-35 psi
70°	35-40 psi
75°	35-45 psi
80°	40-50 psi
85°	45-55 psi
90°	45-55 psi
95°	50-55 psi
100°	50-55 psi
105°	50-55 psi
110°	50-55 psi

on. This will prevent accidental piercing of the R-134a can.

The kit should come with a table showing the desired pressure in your A/C system for the ambient temperature when you do the work.

Turn on the engine, turn your car's A/C system on high, and open the valve on the kit's refrigerant can. Let the can charge the system until the pressure falls within the recommended range on the pressure/temperature table (using the temp where you are doing the work as the figure for reference). Here, our gauge says 40, which is what we wanted. (Note: We tilted the can for this photo of the kit and gauge, but you want the can generally upright as you release the coolant into your car's system.) When you reach the desired pressure, turn the valve on the can closed and remove the connector. If your car's connector had a cap, replace it. Your A/C should now be cold.

Replacing the Antenna

 Skill Level: easy to intermediate

 Tools/Supplies Required: wrench, replacement antenna

 Time Required: 30 minutes to 1 hour

 Parts Source: auto parts store

 Cost Estimate: $15–$150 (non-powered vs. powered)

Except for the type embedded in the windshield glass, antennas tend to hang out in harm's way by nature. Car washes clobber them, wind pushes on them, kids bend and batter them. Retractable electric antennas escape these fates when not in use, but their moving parts don't last forever.

Sometimes you just have to replace your antenna. You can scour the 'net and ring up the dealerships until you find one just like the original, or you can cruise over to the auto parts shop and pick up a universal replacement. We used a General Motors antenna for a European sedan here, and while we had to make a few modifications, it worked fine because, really, there is not a lot of difference between most metal rods stuck through a hole in the fender and connected by thick wire to your stereo.

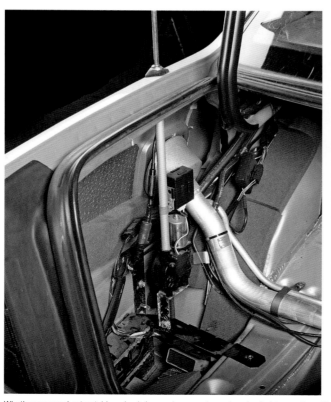

Whether powered-retractable or basic/manual, your antenna is going to have parts on the inside, like connecting hardware and the wire to the radio, and parts outside that secure it to the fender and capture radio waves from the air.

The outside fastener is typically a large nut, which a properly sized wrench can remove with a counterclockwise turn. Inner hardware is also basic; just find the connecting bolt or screw, back it off with a wrench or screwdriver, and then remove it with your fingers, taking care not to drop it.

The connection to the radio is a standard plug on a thick black wire. Pull on each end of the connector to separate the plug from the receptacle. If there are interior panels hiding the lower antenna, look for the screws or plastic fasteners securing them, remove and store them, and take out the panels. (Projects 26, 27, and 32, on popping out a dent, replacing a fender, and replacing a side mirror, show common panel fasteners and how to remove them.)

A power antenna will have an electrical connection to the car's wiring harness. On a modern car, this connector can be pulled apart by hand. If you encounter resistance, there is a tab (sometimes two tabs) holding the connector together. Shine bright light on the connector and you will be able to see whether there is a tab across the connection. If so, you can lift it back with a fingernail and pull the connector apart. (See Project 32 for a photo of this.)

Loosening the nut on the top side of the fender (or other panel bearing the antenna) should allow you to lift the upper part of the antenna mounting hardware free. You can see here the threads protruding from the lower part of the antenna to which the nut on this piece attaches. Once you have the old antenna out, go and buy your replacement so you can compare the old pieces with the new parts.

Rarely will the antenna pass through a body panel that is flat and parallel to the ground. Usually there is some angle, or pitch, to it that the mounting hardware accommodates. Our universal kit came with several different bases of varying wedge shape, and we chose the one closest to leveling out the base. The little plastic prongs that would have dropped into a GM vehicle's mounting hole were too wide for this sedan, so we sawed them off and filed them flat. A hacksaw, with its fine teeth, works fine for this, followed by a flat file or a piece of sandpaper on the ground. (See Project 33—the way we sanded the back of the rearview mirror mounting plate would flatten out these prongs, too, once you sawed off the majority of the prong. This isn't necessary for every antenna swap. Because you brought your old parts and the relevant vehicle to the auto parts store, you can choose an antenna whose new parts fit the existing hole.)

The outer hardware threads onto the inner components. The inner antenna base typically has a pivoting mechanism to accommodate angled panels.

Here's the lower portion of the antenna placed through the body, with rubber mounting gasket—to keep out water—set over it.

Our angled or wedge-shaped exterior base piece sits on the gasket.

A metal nut fits inside the angled base and threads over the lower part of the antenna protruding through the sheet metal.

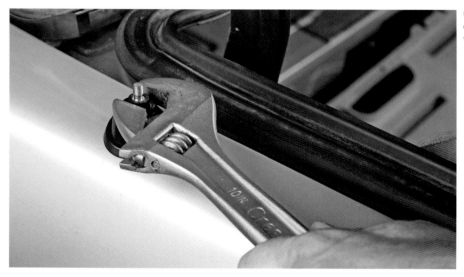

Give this nut a turn with a wrench to snug it down—but don't crank it too hard or you'll break the plastic base.

Our kit used a fixed (as opposed to collapsible) antenna that threaded on. We tightened it a bit with a wrench to keep it secure.

Plug in the antenna wire—if your reception is no good, you probably forgot this part! If you're replacing your old antenna with a power model, you'll need a connection to electrical power too.

Finally, if you removed interior panels for access to the antenna, replace these and secure them with their original fasteners.

PROJECT 39
Repairing a Sticking Power Window

 Skill Level: intermediate

 Tools/Supplies Required: screwdrivers or Allen wrenches, shop light, pivoting mirror, plastic sheeting, shop vac, spray lubricant

 Time Required: 45 minutes–1.5 hours

 Parts Source: auto parts store, salvage yard

 Cost Estimate: $0–$100 if you replace the window motor

Vehicle windows capable of being raised and lowered are guided by tracks inside the door cavity. Over the years, dirt, grunge and rust can accumulate on these parts and create friction that causes windows to slow down or jam. Failure of a power window's electric motor or electricity supply will also render it inoperable.

If the window does nothing when you hit the switch, the electric motor may have failed. A blown fuse or a bad switch (either the master switch that is controlled by the driver or the individual one at the inoperable window) will also interrupt power, as will damaged wiring. The wires are subject to stress and wear in the places where they run between the body and door. (Another possibility: If the window works with the driver's master switch, but not with the individual door's switch, it could be a child protection system. Your owner's manual will tell you how to activate and de-activate that feature.) Regardless of the problem, repairing a malfunctioning power window can be a lot easier to do than you might think.

Our vehicle came out of Arizona, where years of desert dust had penetrated deep within the door and contaminated the grease that lubricates the track that the apparatus holding the window glass moves up or down upon. As a result, the motor labored and the window moved slowly. Replacing a bad motor would be similar to what we did, except that you would unbolt the motor, unplug its wiring, and slip it out of the adjacent hole in the inner door panel. Some styles have a cable system, which would also need to come out.

The passenger rear window on this Ford Explorer moved slowly.

To get at the problem, we need to remove the door trim panel, beginning with the visible fasteners. Our vehicle used Phillips-head screws, but Allen bolts and other styles are common too. Place each fastener you remove in a clean spot, grouping together those taken from the same area.

The door handle is attached to the inner mechanicals and therefore must either be removed or passed through the door trim panel. In this design, a small panel pops out to create a gap large enough for the panel to slip over the handle.

This piece has a thin portion and must be handled carefully to avoid breaking it. Taking your time always makes repair jobs go more smoothly.

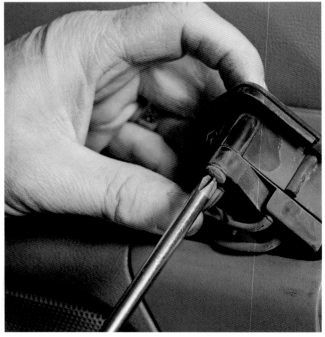

The power window switch will be connected to the motor inside the door. To get the trim panel off, we need to pop out the switch and disconnect the wires.

If you can't see screws around the outside of the trim panel (as were present with our vehicle in Project 26), the panel likely pops off. We used a wide-blade screwdriver and inserted a common construction shim behind it to avoid scratching the paint. Get your fingers behind the panel and pull carefully, dislodging the bottom first.

Continue around the door, pulling out the fasteners. If you encounter strong resistance, stop and study the situation—there may be one or more anchor screws remaining. These are common by speakers and arm rests, for example.

The final maneuver to remove this Ford panel is to lift upward. It hooks over the top of the inner door. Door panels with a lock button emerging from the top will likely need to be lifted upward to clear the rod after you unscrew and remove the button itself.

A plastic-film barrier will cover the door beneath the trim panel. We will need to peel this back to get at the door's inner components.

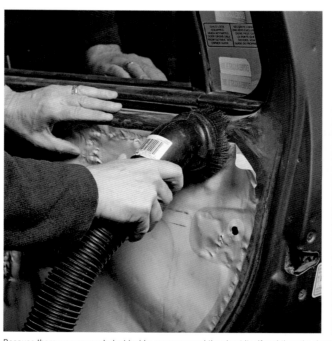

Because there was so much dust inside, we vacuumed the sheet itself and then the door behind it. Dust can interfere with mechanical and electrical parts, so remove it whenever you can.

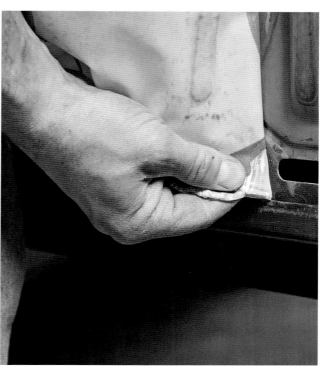

The speaker grille sat over the plastic, so we removed it with an appropriately sized socket wrench. Adhesive holds the plastic to the door. Pull evenly to overcome the adhesive and peel back the film. If you destroy the plastic removing it, you can replace it with ordinary plastic sheeting—for example, drop-cloth material.

This large cavity provided us with access to the inner window workings. A handy pivoting mirror allowed us to peer inside, bouncing shop light in and reflecting a clear view of the parts back to our eyes. These mirrors are inexpensive and available at virtually any auto parts store.

We thoroughly wiped off the inner track using a rag with degreaser on it, then applied a spray lubricant, moving the window up and down periodically to disperse it. As we did this, the window began to move smoothly. Because the lubricant we used is lighter than grease, we may need to reapply it at some point. Grease would last longer, but offer more resistance and, in a dusty climate, become contaminated again.

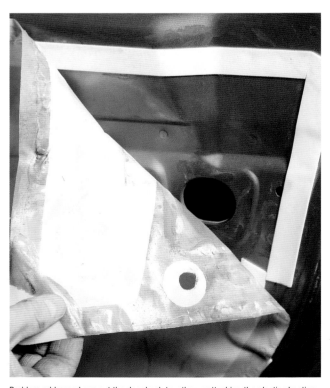

Problem addressed, we put the door back together, reattaching the plastic sheeting with double-sided foam adhesive. You could use a spray adhesive too; just avoid getting it on moving parts.

Remember to line up the lock button, if your vehicle has one, before trying to pop the trim panel back on.

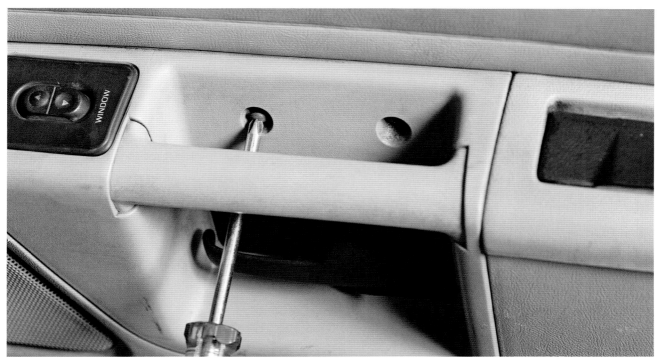

Reinstall all fasteners to their original places.

Once you've reassembled something, clean it up well as a finishing touch on your handiwork.

PROJECT 40
Repairing a Broken Trunk Lock

 Skill Level: easy/intermediate

 Tools/Supplies Required: screwdriver, wrench, replacement lock

 Time Required: 30–60 minute

 Parts Source: dealer, salvage yard, eBay

Cost Estimate: $100–$400

Locks have gotten more complicated on modern vehicles, with electronics supplementing and sometimes substituting for the basic metal key. This complexity brings a higher price tag when a lock breaks.

The trunk lock on our project vehicle was jammed. The key would go only part way in due to some abuse or vandalism. Internal parts in the cylinder that receives the key were damaged beyond repair. As a result, the trunk would not open with the metal key or electronics—it had broken in the locked position.

A dealership could swap out the damaged lock with a new one manufactured by the factory to accept our factory key based on serial number. That cost was quoted at about $400. The same factory-tailored part could be delivered for owner installation for around $260. We fixed it for $100, buying a complete factory lockset, with keys, off eBay for $88 plus shipping. If the cylinder (key receptacle) had been OK on our lock, we could have bought a used lock from a wrecking yard and swapped it in. With that part broken, we needed a key along with the replacement lock!

This Audi electronic trunk lock was jammed in the locked position. Because the key would not go in, we replaced the whole lock mechanism.

Opening the trunk required crawling in with the back seat folded down and hitting the emergency release (many cars will have a release by the driver's controls). Next step is to remove the trunk panel to expose the part and connections.

Any plastic lights or parts holders attached to the outside of the trunk-lid liner must be removed.

This liner is screwed in around the periphery. Remove all fasteners and place them in a clear spot.

The liner may have a lip, in addition to fasteners, that holds it in place. Look for a handhold and pull carefully to see if it will come free. If not, check for some fastener you've missed.

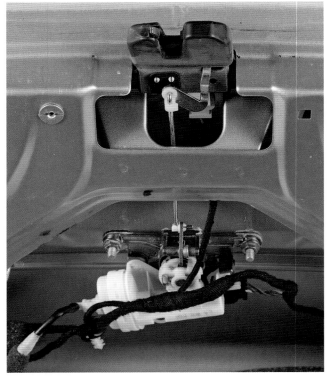

This lock has two main components—a locking mechanism and a separate latch connected and operated with a rod.

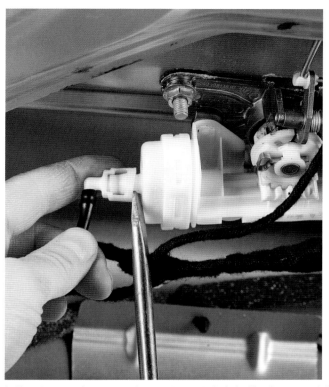

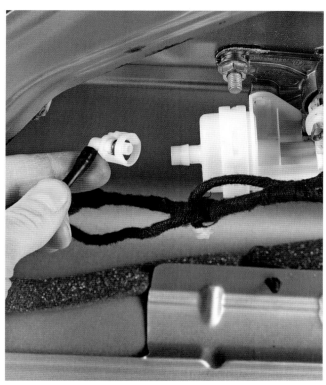

Audi's system uses air pressure and vacuum to operate the locks. Therefore you must disconnect both the pneumatic and electrical unions. For the former, gently separate the air line with a screwdriver.

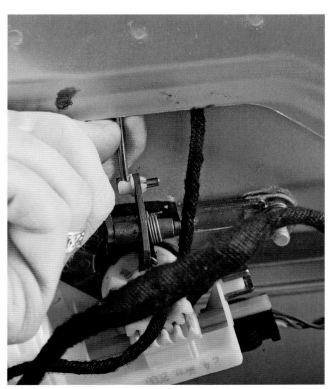

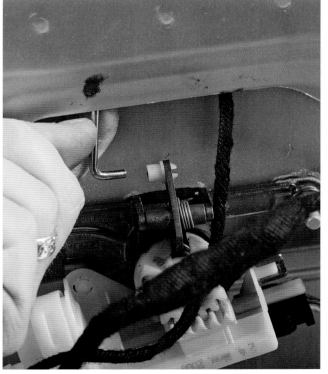

If the lock attaches to the latch with a rod, separate that connection. This one pulls free; look closely to see whether yours fastens in a different way.

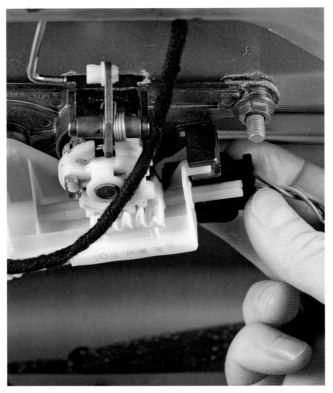

Separate the electrical connector. If it resists, check for a security tab holding the connection together and gently lift it free of whatever tooth or groove it locks into.

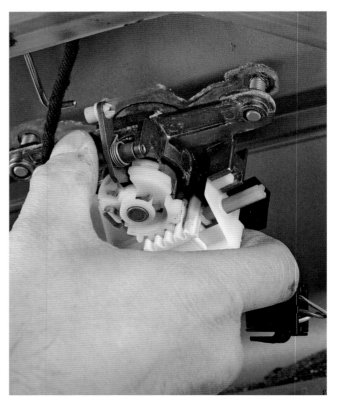

Remove the mounting nuts or bolts and take out the lock.

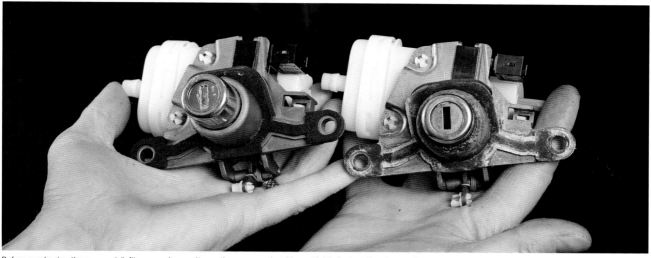

Before purchasing the new part (left), we made sure it was the same as the old one (right). Parts sellers frequently use serial numbers, and always use the make, model, and year to assure compatibility.

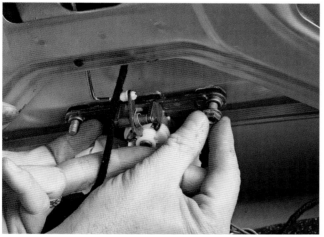

Fit the new part and tighten the mounting nuts/bolts.

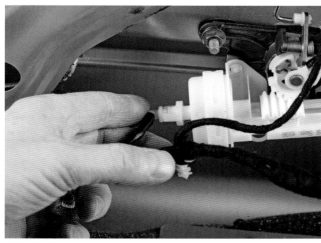

Reattach pneumatic line (if present) and electrical wiring.

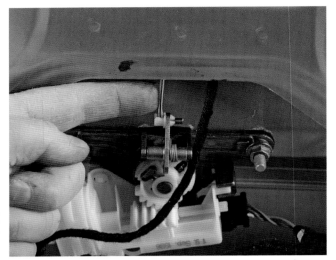

Re-connect the lock-to-latch rod, if present.

Finally, re-fit the trunk liner and any lights or parts-holders that attach to it.

Index

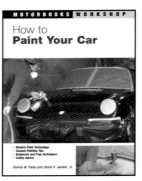

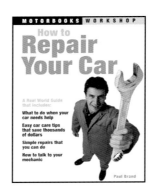